Super Excel

For Dealership Management

Super Excel

For Dealership Management

by
Jack Ross

Published by SmilingEagle Press
For information:
SmilingEagle Press
4327 S Hwy 27 PMB 601
Clermont, FL 34711
www.smilingeagle.com

ISBN: 9798871240526

Printed in the United States of America

Acknowledgments

First, my thanks to Sandi Jerome. Through a fortuitous meeting at NADA years ago, we ended up partnering on many projects, including the Expense Master, the Super DOC, her financial statement workbooks, and of course, this book. Sandi had already begun working on her contribution to the book with this title, and we then began collaborating on the final version. Due to her extensive network through her consulting company and her DMSDealerStar, Grayfox Software was able to get my work out to a wider audience than would have been possible otherwise.

Also, my thanks to Pat and Annie Flaherty of Envisage Group. Through their friendship and collaboration on hardware and software projects, we built some cool stuff, and it allowed me to stretch my programming and Excel skills a little further.Also, to the various managers over the years, including Donna Brower, Dan Pyle, TJ DiSanto, Wendy Bayle, and others who recognized my desire to create software solutions that helped make the dealership a more efficient and more informed company. This book is a small reflection of what I've been able to do and contains some simplified examples of applications I've built for them and others over the years.

A special thanks to my editor at SmilingEagle Press, Cathy Phillips who helped me get "inline."

Super Excel

For Dealership Management

Contents

About Super Excel for Dealerships

Welcome to *Super Excel for Dealership Management*. As I mentioned in the Acknowledgments, this is an updated revision of an Excel book that Sandi Jerome and I had published years ago. Sandi's contribution to the book dealt mostly with interacting with the DMS in order to bring data into Excel and then to process it in various ways, including advanced pivot tables. Because DMS companies change their database and data extraction processes over time, that content was removed from this book version, while this updated version deals mostly with Excel formula basics, more advanced spreadsheet functions, and programming in the Excel VBA environment.

Excel itself has changed radically since the previous version of this book was published. For years it felt like the various Excel tools, functions, etc. remained mostly unchanged, except for different interface improvements with new versions. However, Microsoft has continued to make vast changes and improvements in Excel, to the point where it's difficult now to keep up with new functions, new data tools and methods, and Excel's ability to connect to a wide range of other programs and data, including the web. And AI? That's a whole 'nother world altogether. Between Excel's continued incorporation of AI tools directly into it, and new AI platforms coming out constantly, AI will continue to transform how we work with software today, including Excel.

This book is written to provide you, the user of Excel, with practical help in using this application in your company. While the principles that follow can apply to any general-use purpose, the examples and case studies are geared toward common vehicle dealership procedures.

I've found that people who use Excel often fall into one of four broad categories:

1) 😰 The uncomfortable user. This may or may not be a newbie in the sense that they're new to Excel, but they generally are uncomfortable with using aspreadsheet, or they may be somewhat comfortable but limit themselves to the most basic features and tools available in Excel. As one author once characterized a certain type of technophobe: "These are the users who secretly add up their Excel lists with a calculator." This is not to belittle or make light of someone who is unfamiliar or uncomfortable with using a spreadsheet; it's merely a humorous observation about the way some people approach it. They open a spreadsheet and see this vast screen of little cells with rows and columns, menu options, toolbars, status bars, cryptic icons and more, and it can all be overwhelming. They may know enough to do what someone showed them how to do (whether it's right or wrong), or they may try to accomplish

something and quickly become frustrated. Then they grab their hand calculators and add the numbers up themselves. And why not? Without sufficient exposure and practice, it's easier to use a calculator. It's familiar and it's quick (although not nearly as quick as summing numbers in Excel. In a race between using a hand calculator versus Excel adding even two numbers, I'll put my money on Excel every time).

2) The comfortable user. This is a person who has either used a spreadsheet for some time, or who may intuitively take to it right away. This person generally knows his or her way around the spreadsheet, knows what many or most of the menu items and toolbars are for, and can move quickly and comfortably through many spreadsheet tasks. They may not know what many of the advanced tools built into Excel can do, and they may not be familiar with VBA, the programming language of Excel. Nevertheless, they can build and use basic spreadsheets that can get the job done, efficiently or otherwise.

3) The power user. You may or may not have one of these in your dealership, but if you do, they're generally the person that everybody comes to with questions about using Excel or building solutions with spreadsheets. They are quite comfortable with this application and can often build spreadsheets that are designed for end-users. These may include features

such as data validation, conditional formatting, protected sheets or ranges, charts, pivot tables, linking formulas, and so on. When it comes to VBA, they may run the gamut from complete novice to fairly sophisticated, but generally are somewhere in between. Their spreadsheets therefore may often include some programming that makes the spreadsheet easier to use or more powerful.

4) The developer (sometimes known affectionately or otherwise as "the geek"). It's unlikely that you'll have one of these in the dealership, but it's possible. These are the ones who know how to wring much of the true power out of Excel. Their spreadsheets and VBA programs are often quite professional and may involve a level of automation that can astound lesser mortals. This type often works freelance or for a consulting or programming company and can create custom-made spreadsheets based on a client's needs.

So...which one are you? People usually fall somewhere in the range of these categories rather than squarely in the middle of one. Perhaps you have used Excel for some time and know how to handle basic tasks such as entering simple formulas, basic formatting and so on, but would like to learn more without having to trudge through one of those 600-page 10-pound books you see in the bookstore. Perhaps you realize your job or someone else's in the dealership could be made more efficient or easier if only there was a spreadsheet thatcould help speed that job up. Perhaps you would like to take your spreadsheets just a little further, such as creating a set of spreadsheets that link to a master workbook so that others could enter their information and have it flow to you automatically. Perhaps a department manager or the GM would like something with charts or more concise summary information. This book is designed to helpyou get started in that direction.

We'll be examining two case studies in this book:

The first is the Car Inventory Summary. This workbook will draw information from a downloaded report from the DMS, then automatically format the report and add formulas for additional information not provided in the DMS download.

The second is the Gross Book Analysis. This workbook will use information from a gross book report file and allow the end-user to view and analyze the performance of the salespeople. We'll also begin building a salesperson commission workbook which will allow us to enter our commission information in an efficient way by building a workbook with a good foundation and flexibility.

Also included is a bonus workbook. This is a macro-enabled version of the commission workbook that allows the user to save each salesperson's commission sheet as a PDF file that can then be distributed physically or emailed to the recipient.

Along the way, we'll be covering some topics that will hopefully enlighten you as to some of the capabilities of Excel. We'll touch on the idea of "superformulas", handy formulas such as OFFSET and multiple-condition AND/OR statements, how to use arrays in formulas, quick little tips on Excel shortcuts, and more.

Incidentally, if you wish to learn more about the DMS side, including download procedures, data extraction and import routines, you can check out Sandi's Super Controller series on Amazon; search on Sandi Jerome, or with the link at our publisher's website at https://www.smilingeagle.com/. To find links to all the spreadsheets used in this book visit her website at https://sandijerome.com. Click on the Free e-book link.

So let's get started.

Formulas

"If A is success in life, then A equals x plus y plus z. Work is x, y is play; and z is keeping your mouth shut."
-   Albert Einstein

Note:
For this chapter, the screenshots have accompanying figure numbers. The formula_examples.xlsx file contains tabs with the corresponding figure numbers, so that you can examine the screenshot examples more closely.

Everybody uses the term "formula" (including me),but the more correct term is "function". What's a function? It's an equation that returns a value. And the more you know about functions, the more powerful your spreadsheets can be.

I have a coffee cup in my office with the words "Excel Guru" on one side. On the other side are the words:

"Isn't it obvious? Use the =TRIM(MID(A2,FIND(" ",A2),25)) function and then do a Paste-Special Values. Duh!"

I kind of like that cup. And while most peoples' eyes would glaze over to look at a function like that typed into a spreadsheet cell, believe it or not, it does have its purposes. Most Excel users who do anything with functions will know what something like =SUM(A2:A4) means, and that's a good example of what a function does: it returns a value. If you have the numbers 1,2 and 3 in cells A2, A3, and A4, that function entered into cell A5 (or any cell, for that matter) will *return* the number 6 in the cell. It's an equation, a formula, a function that acts upon the cells referred to, and gives you the answer in the cell in which it's entered.

	A	B
1		
2	1	
3	2	
4	3	
5	=SUM(A2:A4)	
6		

Figure 1.1

The =SUM function is one of the most basic, but there are many, *many* functions built into Excel that work with basic and higher-level math, sophisticated financial, scientific, statistical, text, time and date, database information and more. And in the event you can't find or build an Excel function that suits your needs, you can even create your own user-defined functions.

Useful Excel Functions

`=SUM`

This is probably the workhorse of Excel functions. In any empty cell, you can type `=SUM({first cell in range}:{last cell in range})`. When you press Enter, Excel will sum the total of the numbers in that range. See the explanation of functions above for an example.

Side Point

You can quickly find the sum of a range by highlighting the range with your mouse. Look down at the status bar of Excel on the right-hand side. You'll see "Sum= {whatever}". This is a quick way to see the total without having to create the SUM function. You can also right-click the Sum area on your status bar, and a list of available functions will appear. If you want to see the count of a range, or average, or minimum number, for example, instead of the Sum, simply select that choice with your mouse. The chosen function will remain in Excel until you change it again.

You can also quickly sum a range by clicking in a cell just below a range, then double-clicking the AutoSum button on your toolbar.

Σ ˅

This will automatically sum the range for the first to last contiguous set of cells Excel finds. For example, if you have the number 1 in cell A1, and the numbers 1,2 and 3 in cells A5,A6, and A7, if you go to cell A8 and double-click the AutoSum button, Excel will automatically enter the function `=SUM(A5:A7)` for you.

Because there's at least one empty cell between A1 and A5, Excel won't grab the number in A1 and include it in the function.

Divide, Multiply, Add, and Subtract functions

You can use the basic math functions above by simply referring to the cells you want to calculate and entering the function symbol. For example, if you wish to multiply the values in cells A2 and A3, in an open cell you would simply type =A2*A3. The same applies with division (/), addition (+) and subtraction (-). Using these math symbols, you can create a formula involving any number of cells, up to 256 characters in length.

Side Point

Order of precedence. Just like in basic math, if you're doing multiple calculations involving multiple symbols, you'll need to create your formula with parentheses to set your order of precedence. This tells Excel which operations to perform first. For example, if you want to add the contents of A2 and A3, then multiply the result by what's in A4, you could type =A2+A3*A4, but that would give you an incorrect answer. If 1 was in A2, 2 was in A3, and 3 was in A4, your formula would return 7, because Excel is correctly multiplying 2 times 3, then adding the 1 to get 7. Your formula should be entered as =(A2+A3)*A4, which would return 9. Excel sees the parentheses and correctly does the addition first, then multiplies the result by what's in A4.

Relative versus Absolute

This can be a tough concept until you get familiar with it. It has to do with the way spreadsheets think about the cells referred to in a formula. If you have numbers in A1 and A2, and in A3 type =SUM(A1:A2), you'll get the sum of those two numbers. Now, if you press Ctrl-C to copy that formula, go to another cell, say C3, and press Enter or Ctrl-V to paste the formula, that formula will now correctly say =SUM(C1:C2) and sum the two cells above if there are any numbers in them.

	A	B	C	D	E
1	15		22		
2	45		72		
3	=SUM(A1:A2)		94		
4					
5					
6					
7					
8					
9		Formula copied and pasted from A3			
10		to C3 gives the correct answer			
11					

Figure 1.2

But what's happening in the spreadsheet's 'thinking'? In a formula, Excel is not 'thinking' A1, for example. To Excel, the formula in A3 is really saying "Give me the sum of the cell 2 rows above to the cell 1 row above". Then when you copy and paste that formula to another cell, Excel once again says, in effect, "Give me the sum of the cell 2 rows above to the cell 1 row above", only now it's referring to C1 and C2 instead of A1 and A2.

The formulas are by nature relative to their location, which is why it's so easy to copy and paste a formula from one location to another. But what if you always needed to refer to cell A1 in your formula? For example, what if A1 contains a percentage, like .5, and you need to multiply that by the sum of calculations everywhere in the sheet?

Example: as shown in figure 1.3, A1 contains .5, A3 contains 4, A4 contains 5, C3 contains 9, C4 contains 7. Place your cursor in cell A5 and enter the formula: `=SUM(A3:A4)*A1`. Excel will return 4.5, because it's adding A3 and A4, then multiplying the result by .5. Now, with A5 still the current cell, press Control-C to copy the formula, then go to C5 and press Enter to paste. What happened? You get zero.

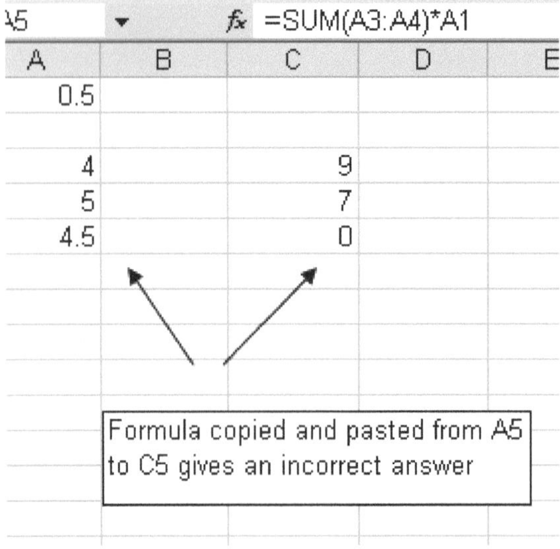

Figure 1.3

Why? Because Excel says, in effect, add what's in the range 2 cells above me down to 1 cell above me (C3 and C4 in this case), then multiply the result by what's in the cell 4 rows above me." But there's nothing in C1, the cell 4 rows above the copied formula. You WANTED to multiply the results by what's in A1, but because the formula is relative to its location, Excel simply moved its reference from A1 to C1, just like it did with the other two cell references in the formula.

That's where the absolute reference comes in. Go back to A5 and press F2 to edit the formula. Now, with your cursor near the "A1" part of the formula, press F4. You'll see dollar signs appear beside the A and the 1. Now press Enter to save the formula. Press Ctrl-C to copy, go to C5 and press Enter to paste. What happens? You get 8 instead of 0. Look at the formula in C5. The sum numbers refer to column C, but the $A$1 stayed the same. The dollar signs are absolute reference placeholders, "locking" Excel into always referring to A1, which is what you want.

A5   ▾ f_x =SUM(A3:A4)*$A$1

A	B	C	D	E
0.5				
4		9		
5		7		
4.5		8		

Formula copied and pasted from A5 to C5 gives a correct answer with absolute reference to A1

Figure 1.4

If you're still in C5 (or A5), press F2 again to edit the formula. With your cursor near the $A$1, press F4 again. Then again. Then again. Then again. Each time, you'll see the dollar sign move, disappear, then reappear. Excel allows you to toggle the absolute reference, first locking the reference to $A$1, then A$1, then $A1, then A1. Each time, the lock is effective to the cell only (A1), then to ONLY cell 1, but a relative reference to column A, then the ONLY to column A, but a relative reference to cell 1, and so on. This allows for a great deal of flexibility in choosing what absolute references you want.

Look at the spreadsheet below. Here we see different percentages in A2, A3, and A4. By locking the reference to only column A (as shown in the formula bar above, we can successfully copy and paste this formula from column D to column F.)

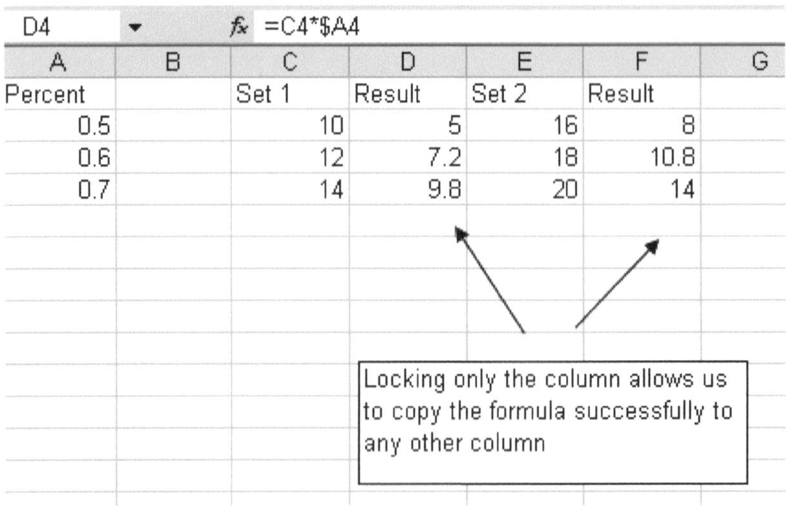

Figure 1.5

=VLOOKUP

This function is also initially hard to come to grips with, but once you do, you'll be surprised at how much you use it. This function looks up a value in another range, based on a reference in the current range, and returns the appropriate value in the lookup range.

For example, look at the spreadsheet below. Here we have a reference section and our data section. The reference section contains a list of counties and their respective rates (tax rates or whatever). The data section contains a list of sales and the customer's corresponding county. We want to look up the customer's county in our reference section and get the corresponding rate, then multiply the sale amount by that for the final number.

	G2		▾		*fx* =VLOOKUP(E2,$A$2:$B$4,2,FALSE)			
	A	B	C	D	E	F	G	H
1	Reference			Customer#	Customer County	Sales	Rate	Total
2	County 1	4.5%		Customer 1	County 2	100.00	4.6%	104.60
3	County 2	4.6%		Customer 2	County 3	124.50	4.7%	130.35
4	County 3	4.7%		Customer 3	County 1	527.25	4.5%	550.98
5								
6								

Figure 1.6

Look at the formula bar. The function:

```
=VLOOKUP(E2,$A$2:$B$4,2,FALSE)
```

is what does the job for us. Here's the explanation of this function:

We want to look up the county in column E and find the rate that corresponds to it. So our function begins: `=VLOOKUP(E2`. Now, where do we want to look it up? In our reference area A2:B4. And because we'll be copying and pasting this function to the entire data range, we'll want to use our absolute reference placeholders, thus the dollar signs. `($A$2:$B$4)`.

Now, the VLOOKUP function uses the left-most column to look up its values, so it will be looking at anything in A2 through A4. We want to return any matching values it finds in column B (i.e., column 2), so our formula at this point says, `=VLOOKUP(E2,$A$2:$B$4,2)`

Technically, that's all we need. If we press Enter at this point, our formula will work. It will look up whatever is in E2 (County 2 in this case) in cells A2 through A4. It will find a match and give us what it finds in column 2 (column B) and return 4.6. We can then use that for further calculations in any other cells, like those in column H.

What's the FALSE part of the statement for? This tells Excel that if there IS no match in column A, then we don't want anything returned. Instead, we'll get an error (#N/A). This is important in most cases, because if we don't put the FALSE portion of the function in, then

Excel will look up the value, not find it, but will then give us the closest match to it. There are times when this is desirable, such as looking up a discount percent and finding the closest match, but not in the case where we're trying to find an exact match to a county rate.

=XLOOKUP (Better than VLOOKUP!)

One of the functions that was added to Excel after the original version of this book was published is XLOOKUP. Once you see how much easier and more powerful it is, you might just begin using it instead of VLOOKUP.

In its simplest form, the function is:
```
=XLOOKUP({value},{lookup array},{return array}).
```

Below is an example that shows one difference between VLOOKUP and XLOOKUP:

Suppose, for example, you have a list of Items, Categories and Values, and you want to find the value of a given category. With VLOOKUP the formula in cell B7 would return 200 for Category B.

| B7 | | | | | | fx | =VLOOKUP(A7,B2:C4,2,FALSE) |

	A	B	C	D	E	F	G	H	I
1	Item	Category	Value						
2	Item 1	Category A	100						
3	Item 2	Category B	200						
4	Item 3	Category C	300						
5									
6	Category Selection	Value							
7	Category B	200							
8									

Figure 1.7

As you can see in the formula bar, the VLOOKUP function looks up the entry in A7 (in this case, Category B) in the range of B2 through C4 and returns the value in the second column.

Now, instead take the same example for Items, Categories, and Values:

| B7 | | | | | | fx | =XLOOKUP(A7,B2:B4,A2:A4) |

	A	B	C	D	E	F	G	H
1	Item	Category	Value					
2	Item 1	Category A	100					
3	Item 2	Category B	200					
4	Item 3	Category C	300					
5								
6	Category Selection	Item						
7	Category B	Item 2						
8								
9								

Figure 1.8

But instead of wanting to return the value for a category, you want to return its corresponding item. How would you do that? You can't use VLOOKUP, because that function works only from left to right.

But with XLOOKUP, that limitation is gone. Notice the XLOOKUP function in the formula bar in the screenshot above:

```
=XLOOKUP(A7,B2:B4,A2:A4)
```

Again, we're looking up the category in cell A7 (Category B), but with XLOOKUP, your lookup range is B2 through B4, and the value you want to find and return is in range A2 through A4. The result? Item 2. As you can see, XLOOKUP can look up not only values to the right, but also left. XLOOKUP is also more efficient, because you only need to refer to the range you're looking up and the range you're returning. If you had a data table with 20 columns in it, for example, with VLOOKUP you would need to include the entire table, depending on the columns you're looking up and returning, but with XLOOKUP you need only the two columns.

One additional option to XLOOKUP that I generally prefer to include is the argument {if not found}. Referring to figure 1.8, the XLOOKUP function would now be:

```
=XLOOKUP(A7,B2:B4,A2:A4,"Item Not Found")
```

With that additional parameter, if you had an incorrect or missing category in A7, the function would return "Item Not Found" (or whatever you would enter for the parameter).

=OFFSET and =SUM(OFFSET)

The OFFSET and SUM(OFFSET) functions are, again, somewhat difficult to grasp at first, but are great little ingenious functions that come in handy when building your spreadsheets.

To provide a practical example of the OFFSET and SUM(OFFSET) functions, a complete sample workbook, named offset_example.xlsx, is included that illustrates these formulas in a budget workbook. The workbook consists of 4 tabs: Actual_vs_Budget, Budget_Table, CurrYr_Table, and PriorYr_Table. These last 3 are sheets that contain our numbers, and the Actual_vs_Budget sheet examines those numbers using the OFFSET formulas.

(Because this section deals with a separate workbook, we won't use illustration numbers. But we'll pick back up with them when we get to the next section.)

In cell C6, notice the formula in the formula bar:
```
=OFFSET(PriorYr_Table!$C6,0,5,1,1)
```

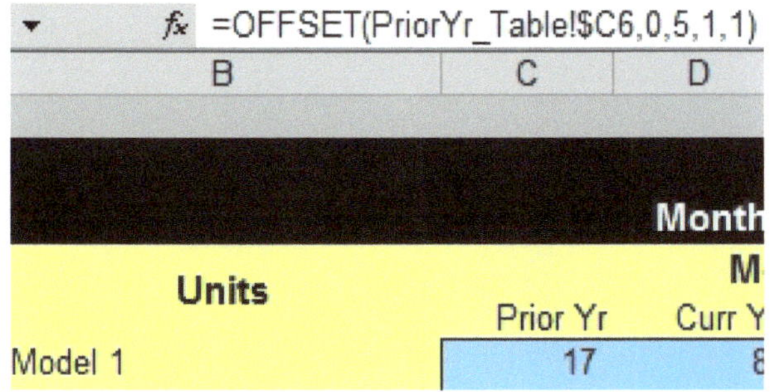

...which returns a value of 17 in this case. If we looked at the PriorYr_Table and looked at cell C6, we would see our Model 1 name there:

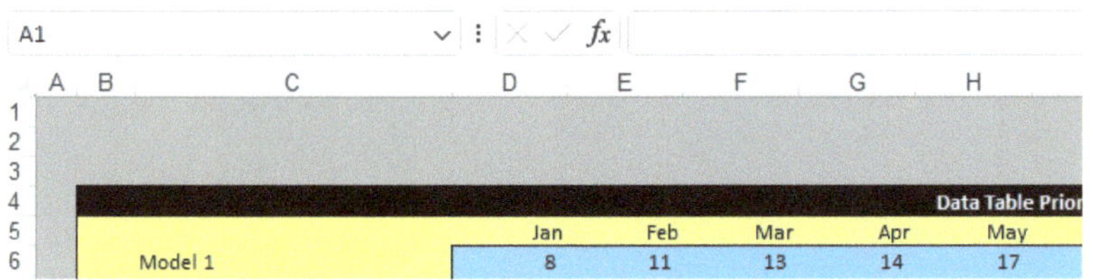

What the OFFSET formula does is this:

The first part (PriorYr_Table!$C6) is the reference area the formula needs. Here we can see were referencing cell C6 in the PriorYr_Table.

The second part (0) returns the number of rows we want to reference from our current location. In this case, we want 0 rows, meaning we want to refer to our current row.

The third part, 5, is the number of columns we want to reference from our current location. In this case, we want 5 rows from our current location.

The last two numbers represent our height and width, which we would use if we're trying to return a value contained in more than one cell (this is less common in OFFSET, but necessary when using SUM(OFFSET)). Generally we're trying to return the value in a single cell.

So, in this example our formula is saying, in effect, "Give me the value in the PriorYr_Table starting in cell C6, 0 rows down and 5 rows over." The correct answer is returned: 17.

The other formulas on the Month side of the sheet are similar, referring to the other tabs for the Budget and Current Year information.

Now notice the Year-To-Date side of the sheet. The formula in G6 is:

```
=SUM(OFFSET(PriorYr_Table!$C6,0,1,1,5))
```

	fx =SUM(OFFSET(PriorYr_Table!$C6,0,1,1,5))				
B	**C**	**D**	**E**	**F**	**G**
		Budget Comparison			
		Month: 5		**Year:**	**2009**
Units		**Month**			
	Prior Yr	Curr Yr	Budget	Variance	Prior Yr
Model 1	17	8	13	(5)	63

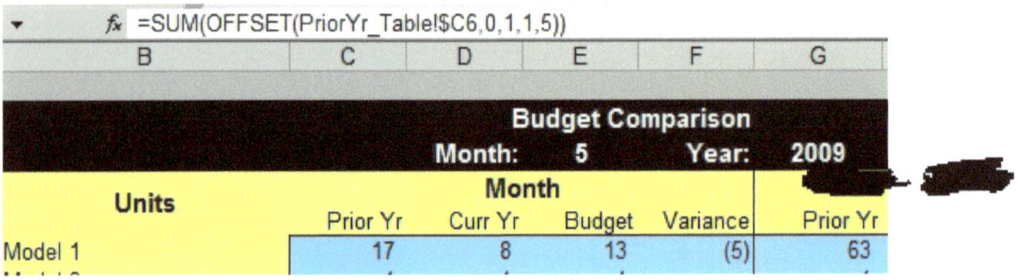

Here we combine the SUM function with the OFFSET function. Our formula is saying, in effect, "Give me the sum of the PriorYr_Table, starting with cell C6, 0 rows down (0), one column to the right (1), with a height of one cell and a width of 5 cells."

Our OFFSET formula starts with column D and adds up the numbers in the next 5 columns, returning 63. The other formulas in the Year-To-Date area are also similar.

Using the OFFSET and SUM(OFFSET) formulas in this way, we're able to examine the correct monthly and year-to-date numbers for our Budget, Current Year, and Prior Year data. Let's make one improvement. Notice how we've changed the formula on the Actual_vs_Budget page for C6:

=OFFSET(PriorYr_Table!$C6,0,Sel_Mon,1,1)

	C6	▼		*fx*	=OFFSET(PriorYr_Table!$C6,0,Sel_Mon,1,1)

	A	B	C	D	E
1					
2					Budge
3				Month:	5
4		Units			Month
5				Prior Yr	Curr Yr	Bu
6	Model 1			17	8

Notice we've changed the 5 to "Sel_Mon". This is a name we've created for cell E3, which contains our month. (If you're not familiar with named ranges, we'll be discussing that in our case studies). We've also modified cell E3 to use a list in Data Validation. If you click your mouse in E3, then click the Data tab, then Data Validation, you can see that we've allowed a list, and in the Source box we've entered 1,2,3,4,5,6,7,8,9,10,11,12. This forces the cell to allow only those entries. By referencing this cell (with the name Sel_Mon) in our OFFSET formulas then, our formulas will all update automatically whenever we change the value in cell E3. We can review any month from January through December, simply by changing the number in cell E3. Once you become comfortable with the OFFSET formula, you'll find uses for it that will make your spreadsheets much more efficient.

Formulas to work with text

Excel has quite a few functions that allow you to work with and manipulate text. With these you can break up and combine text, extract portions of text from cells, change capitalization, and more. Why would you be concerned with these kinds of functions? Because there are many situations where you have to work with text data from your DMS.

For example, say you've done a download of customer names and addresses that you want to do a mailing for. The downloaded spreadsheet has names in the form: LAST NAME, FIRST NAME. You want to be able to format these names in the form: First Name Last Name, with the first and last name capitalized and the rest in lower case, and obviously with no comma. How would you do that in Excel?

Look at the example below:

B1	▼	f_x =RIGHT(A1,LEN(A1)-FIND(",",A1)-1)			
	A	B	C	D	E	F
1	SMITH, JOHN	JOHN				

figure 1.9

Here we have SMITH, JOHN in our downloaded file. The function:

```
=RIGHT(A1,LEN(A1)-FIND(",",A1)-1)
```

in cell B1 returns our customer's first name. How does this work?

This works by combining several functions: RIGHT, LEN, and FIND. The first thing we need to do is extract the customer's first name, so we use the RIGHT function, because the customer's name is in the right portion of the cell. This function needs to know what we want the right OF (in this case, the contents of A1), and how many characters of that right portion we want. The trouble is, we don't KNOW how many characters we want, because the customer's first name can be any number of characters, depending on which cell we're working on. So, to find the correct number of characters, we use the function LEN. This gives us the length of whatever cell we're examining. SMITH, JOHN will have a length of 11 characters (including the space after the comma).

But we don't want the whole length of what's in A1, we want only the portion that is the customer's first name. So to find *that*, we use the FIND function. In this function, we specify what we want to find, in this case, the comma in cell A1. If we typed only the FIND function in cell B1: `FIND(","  A1)`, Excel would return 6, because the comma is the 6th character in the cell.

So by combining these functions, Excel says, in effect, "Give me the right portion of A1. But I only want the right portion of whatever the length of A1 is MINUS the point where it finds the comma." Excel finds the comma at position 6. The length of the cell is 11. So 11 minus 6 is 5. Excel thus returns the last 5 characters of A1, which is " JOHN".

But notice the space in front of JOHN. This is because there's a space after the comma. We don't want that. So to get rid of it, we add one more wrinkle to our function. The "-1" at the end says, "Before you return those last characters at the right of the cell (" JOHN" in this case), subtract 1 character" (the space). When the function completes its examination, it returns a nice, clean "JOHN" as the result.

Now, we need to extract the customer's last name in the left portion of the cell. That part's easy. We use the function `=LEFT(A1,FIND(",",A1)-1)`. This function extracts the left portion of A1 by finding the comma (at position 6, remember), and giving us everything to the left of it. But because Excel also counts the comma, we again need to remove it by using our "-1" parameter. When it's all said and done, we end up with "SMITH", just as we want it.

C1	▼	*fx*	=LEFT(A1,FIND(",", A1)-1)	
	A	B	C	D	E
1	SMITH, JOHN	JOHN	SMITH		
2					

Figure 1.10

Now, how do can we combine the results into First Name Last Name? Because we have our portions extracted, we can now recombine them into whatever format we want. So D1 contains =B1 & " " & C1. This takes whatever is in cell B1 (customer's first name), adds a space, then adds whatever is in cell C1 (customer's last name.) The result is JOHN SMITH.

D1	▼	*fx*	=B1 & " " & C1	
	A	B	C	D
1	SMITH, JOHN	JOHN	SMITH	JOHN SMITH
2				

Figure 1.11

What if we want it with proper case? By using the Excel PROPER function, we can also do that automatically. If we replace our function with:

`=PROPER (B1 & " " &C1)`, our result will be John Smith. There. Ready for mail merge.

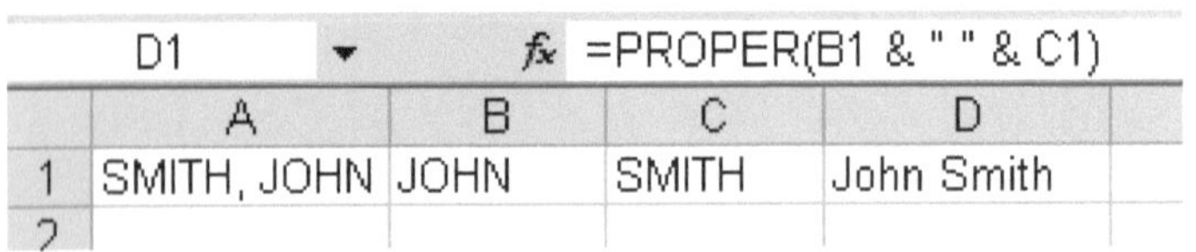

Figure 1.12

Superformulas

The above example uses several steps to break apart and recombine the cell into the format we want. But by combining the functions further and further, a user can create a superformula. Superformulas are good, in that they can kill a lot of birds with one stone, so to speak. Instead of having our functions span 3 columns, like they do in the example above, we COULD use one formula:

```
=PROPER(RIGHT(A1,LEN(A1)-FIND(",",A1)-1)&"
"&LEFT(A1,FIND(",",A1)-1))
```

Figure 1.13

...and get the same results in one cell. Pretty cool, huh? If you look closely at the formula above, you'll see that it's nothing more than a combining of the formulas we explained. But now everything is handled in one cell instead of spreading them out across multiple columns.

Here's an example of a really cool superformula: What formula could you use to give us the first and last name for a cell that contains LAST NAME, FIRST NAME, and MAY or MAY NOT contain a middle initial or name after the first name? The example of the superformula above is insufficient, because it will give us the middle initial or name even though we don't want it.

Here's the formula (spanning several lines):

```
=IF(ISERROR(FIND(" ",RIGHT(A2,LEN(A2)-FIND(",",A2)-
1))),RIGHT(A2,LEN(A2)-FIND(",",A2)-1),LEFT(RIGHT(A2,LEN(A2)-
FIND(",",A2)-1),FIND(" ",RIGHT(A2,LEN(A2)-FIND(",",A2)-1))-1))&"
" & LEFT(A2,FIND(",",A2)-1)
```

	Full Name	Position	Final Name
1	Full Name	Position	Final Name
2	Anthony, Salvatore	Porter	Salvatore Anthony
3	Allens, David Joseph	Driver	David Allens

Figure 1.14

Impressive, eh? It took me awhile to put this one together. You'll find that once you do create a superformula that you can re-use for different spreadsheets, you'll want to save it. So you can save a copy of the workbook that contains the formula, or you could begin a workbook that contains a set of superformulas, each with its own worksheet. That way, when you need to reach into your bag of tricks to retrieve your formula, you'll know right where it is.

Okay, we've warmed up by getting familiar with Excel in general, working with functions, and toolbar buttons, and getting an idea of some of Excel's power. Now let's delve into the case studies to see some practical applications.

Keyboard Shortcuts

Oh, one more thing...

This is something that people usually really like or they really hate: Excel keyboard shortcuts. Some people, like me, use them whenever possible. But I've stood beside users while they're trying to show me some problem with their Excel spreadsheet, and as they labor along going back and forth between using the keyboard and mouse, I find myself stifling an anguished cry of "There's a quicker way to do that!" But some of them get irritated when I try to show them, so I've generally learned to keep my mouth shut.

But Excel does have a *ton* of keyboard shortcuts for the spreadsheet environment, and the bottom line is, if you learn some and use them, you will be faster in Excel than by constantly reaching for the mouse. Some of these listed below, like the copy-and-paste shortcuts, formatting shortcuts, and navigation shortcuts, you'll find indispensable if you're prone to using the keyboard.

This is just a sample list. You can find a much more comprehensive list by going to Microsoft Office Online and searching for keyboard shortcuts, and you can also find more sites that list them by typing "Excel keyboard shortcuts" in your browser's search engine.

Super Excel for Dealership Management

General

Description	Shortcut Key
New file	Ctrl + N
Open file	Ctrl + O
Save file	Ctrl + S
Move between open workbooks	Ctrl + F6
Close file	Ctrl + F4
Save as	F12
Display the print menu	Ctrl + P
Select whole spreadsheet	Ctrl + A
Select column	Ctrl + Space
Select row	Shift + Space
Undo last action	Ctrl + Z
Redo last action	Ctrl + Y

Navigating

Description	Shortcut Key
Up one screen	Page Up
Down one screen	Page Down
Move to next worksheet	Ctrl + Page Down
Move to previous worksheet	Ctrl + Page Up
Go to first cell in data region	Ctrl + Home
Go to last cell in data region	Ctrl + End

Formatting Text In Worksheet

Description	Shortcut Key
Bold toggle for selection	Ctrl + B
Italic toggle for selection	Ctrl + I
Underline toggle for selection	Ctrl + U
Apply outline borders	Ctrl + Shift + 7
Remove all borders	Ctrl + Shift + Underline
Wrap text in same cell	Alt + Enter

Copying and Moving Text

Description	Shortcut Key
Cut	Ctrl + X
Copy	Ctrl + C
Paste	Ctrl + V

Inserting Text Automatically

Description	Shortcut Key
Autosum a range of cells	Alt + Equals Sign
Insert the date	Ctrl + ; (semi-colon)
Insert the time	Ctrl + Shift + ; (semi-colon)

Insert columns/rows   Ctrl + Shift + + (plus sign)
Insert a new worksheet   Shift + F11

Misc

Description   Shortcut Key
Find text   Ctrl + F
Replace text dialog   Ctrl + H
Edit a cell comment   Shift + F2
Display the spreadsheet's   Ctrl-~ (Ctrl – tilde)
formulas and constants. (This is a really cool one. Press the Control and tilde key and your spreadsheet will open up to reveal every formula, number, and text entry in the spreadsheet. Good for checking for missing formulas or reviewing them for consistency. To turn off this feature, press Control-tilde again.)

Case Study #1 - DMS data worksheets

Example workbook: car_inv.xlsx

"An efficiency expert is a man hired to introduce short cuts in order to make more time to make out more reports."
        - Anonymous

Many times, we download data from the DMS using utilities like the RXR function in ADP or an ERALink query that allows direct downloads into spreadsheets. These spreadsheets may be far from what we want, though when it comes to final presentation. How can we use Excel to give us our final results?

In this example, we'll be working with a workbook that contains vehicle data. The beginning spreadsheet contains our raw information, but we need it prepared so that it can be printed, and we also want to add a calculated field. Some (most?) dealerships, good, bad or otherwise, prefer paper handouts of the car inventory so that salespeople and managers can look at it (so much for our paperless society).

   The screenshot below shows a trimmed-down version of our downloaded file. The DMS download contains the car inventory sorted by make, then model, then year in descending order. We could have added one or more report break fields on the DMS side (breaks in the report based on changes in make and model, for example), but we're going to let Excel do this for us instead.

	A	B	C	D	E	F	G	H	I	J	K
1	STOCK-NO.	YR	MAKE	MODEL	COLOR	INT-COLOR	SERIAL	MILES	RETAIL	STATUS	ENTRY
2	R0049A	19	HYUN	SONA	X/SILVER	X BLACK	5NPE34AF9KH747493	61899	15,850	S	12-Oct-23
3	N0018A	11	TOYO	SCINXB	X/FLINT	X GRAY	JTLZE4FE9B1125522	196436	6,937	S	14-Oct-21
4	Q0594B	16	DODG	CARAG	X/SILVER	X GRAY	2C4RDGBG5GR314908	104551	12,995	S	19-Nov-23
5	Q0603A	15	JEEP	GRANC	X/BEIGE	X TAN	1C4RJFBG7FC146450	98346	16,350	S	29-Sep-23
6	T166	21	TOYO	PRIUS	X/GOLD	X TAN	JTDL9MFU3M3030334	22145		S	2-Jul-21
7	T174	22	TOYO	TACO	X/GOLD	X TAN	3TMCZ5ANONM494987	11168		S	17-Mar-22
8	T180	23	TOYO	HIGHLN	X/BAMBO(	X TAN	5TDKDRBH8PS501847	10830		S	20-Dec-22
9	R0013	24	TOYO	CAMR	X/SILVER	X GRAY	4T1G31AK7RU621257	5	32,253	S	29-Aug-23
10	R0037	24	TOYO	TUND	GRAY		5TFLA5DB0RX139140	6	56,868	S	20-Sep-23

So, what do we want the end result to be for this spreadsheet? We want to have breaks (or subtotals to Excel) on make and model. We also want a calculated column at the end that shows how long the vehicle has been in stock, based on its entry date, and we want the report formatted to print 1 page wide by however many pages tall we need.

The first thing we want to do before preparing our report for printing is create our calculated field for aging. We'll start by recording a macro, and then we'll get under the hood to modify it and automate the process for us. The idea is not to have to do all this stuff manually every time we get a new download, which would probably be daily. So, to automate it, we need to record some Excel macros.

A little about Excel macros...

If you've never created an Excel (or Word, or Access, or Reflection, or any VBA) macro before, don't worry. You don't have to be the proverbial rocket scientist. After you follow along with the examples in these case studies, you'll begin to realize it's not too hard at all to create basic macros. If you ever decide to get seriously into it, well, that's a different story. But for our purposes, these examples are easy to create and easy to understand.

A couple of points to keep in mind about working with macros before we get started...

- If you don't see the Developer tab at the top of Excel, you can easily turn that on by clicking File, then Options. In the Excel Options dialog box, click "Customize Ribbon". In the right-hand panel, scroll down until you see Developer, then click the checkbox next to it. Click OK to close the dialog box, and you should now see the Developer tab along with the others.

- If you've never used Excel macros before, either of your own or someone else's creation, you may get a warning message when you open an Excel workbook that contains macros. This is due to Excel's security settings. To modify your settings (if necessary), in Excel click File, then Options. In the Excel Options dialog box, click Trust Center, then the Trust Center Settings button. From there, click Macro Settings, and on the right-side panel, select "Disable VBA macros with notification". Then close Excel and re-open it for the changes to take effect. This will configure Excel to display a button below the ribbon that will prompt you to Enable Content if a workbook is macro-enabled. (And it goes without saying, never click the Enable Content button if you're not sure you can trust a workbook you received from someone).

- Now that we're getting into the subject of Excel macros, everything should work fine when you open the example workbooks referred to in these case studies. The operative word here is *should*. With my previous book, *Advanced ADP Reflection*, I included a Daily Operating Control workbook that dealerships could use as their DOC report. People occasionally contact me with questions about this, including running into problems with the macros. They would sometimes get an "Object not Found" error message and the macro would crash. This kind of problem is not due to the macro itself, but to Excel's references not being correctly loaded.

  If you open any of these sample workbooks and get an error when you run the macros, go into Excel's VBA macro environment by pressing Alt-F11. Then on the menu bar click Tools, then

References. A list of all the various objects (references) available for Excel to use is listed. Most of them will be unchecked, which is fine. Look for any references, usually near the top of the list, which say "Missing". This is generally the culprit whenever a macro crashes with an "Object Not Found" error. This kind of problem is rare, but it happens. Welcome to the world of man-made computer applications.

Now back to our example.

First of all, let's open the car_inv_before.xlsx workbook. This is our starting point, the workbook that's created from the DMS download. From here we'll begin creating our code in VBA.

To record a macro, you can click the Developer tab, then Record Macro.

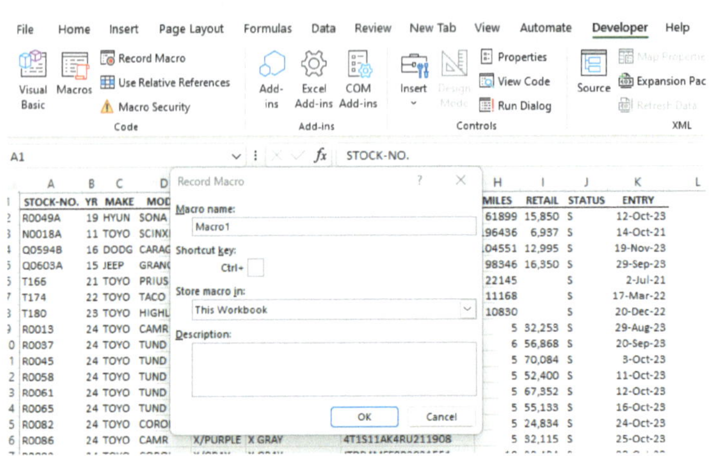

The Record Macro dialog box will appear. Assign the new macro a meaningful name, such as PrepareVehReport or something similar (just no spaces in the name, please).

There is also a prompt for where to store this new macro. Because this spreadsheet is going to be brand-new every time it's downloaded from the DMS, we can't store it in this workbook or else we'll lose our macro next time we download the file. So instead, click the dropdown box and select Personal Macro Workbook. For the description, you can either leave it as it is, or put a short blurb about the purpose of the macro. Then click OK and you're ready to go. We're now in VBA record mode. Everything you do while the recorder is running is being captured in this macro.

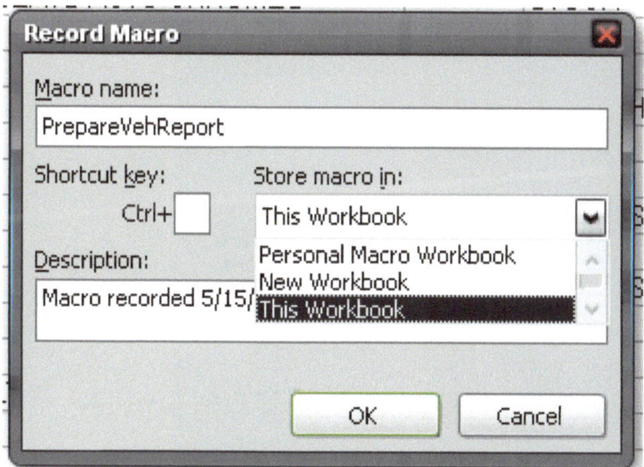

Side Point

In the Record Macro dialog box there's also a prompt for a shortcut key. What that means is that you can assign your own hotkey to this macro, so that whenever you want to run it, all you need to do is press the hotkey combination. For example, if you typed the letter "r" in that box, once the macro is recorded, you could then press Ctrl-r to run the macro at any time. You could also type an uppercase R, so that you could press Ctrl-Shift-R. It's pretty handy if you have a macro you run on a regular basis. Keep in mind though that any shortcut key you assign will take precedence over any predefined Excel shortcut. For example, if you typed "f" as a shortcut, your macro would take precedence over Excel's Ctrl-f, which is the Find function. The only way you could do a find in Excel after that is by clicking Find and Select on the Home tab.

First, let's click on cell L1, the column just past our entry date (the date the vehicle was put into inventory). Type "Days In Inv" and press Enter. Then go back up to L1 and press Control-B to make the text bold. Then go down to cell L2. Here we type the formula:

```
=NOW()–K2
```

...and press Enter. This formula gives us the number of days between today (now) and the entry date of the vehicle. Next we'll format this cell to show the days in the correct format of zero decimals. Once again click in cell L2, then click Format Cells, then on the Number tab choose Number with 0 decimal places.

Now we're going to copy this formula down one cell to start our copy-and-paste portion. Before we do that, though, we want to make sure of a setting on our Developer tab. Below the Record Macro button is a setting called "Use Relative References". Click that. This will ensure the macro will not refer to hard-coded cells or ranges.

Now with your cursor still in cell L2, press Ctrl-C to copy. Move down to cell L3 and press Ctrl-V to paste.

Okay, we're done with this part of the macro. You can stop the recorder by clicking Stop Recording on the Developer tab. The animated copy marquee will still be moving because we're still in copy-paste mode, so press the Escape key to cancel it. Now let's take a look at our handiwork.

If you press Alt-F11 or click Visual Basic on the Developer tab, you can open the Excel VBA editor. This can be a little intimidating if you've never used it, but it will quickly become familiar. You should see a Project window along either the left or right side. If not, click View on the menu bar and select Project Explorer.

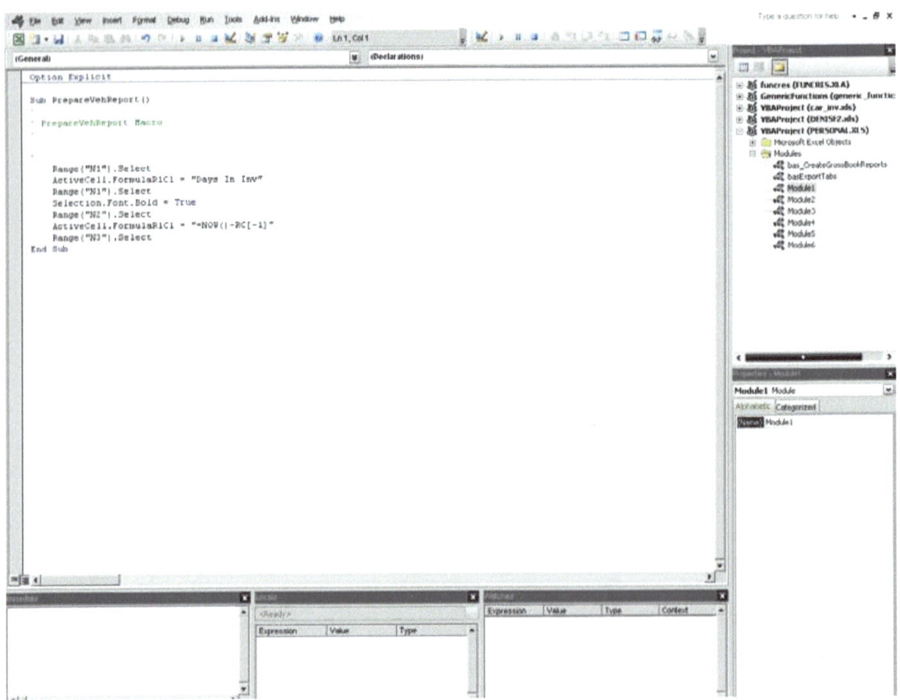

Under the VBAProject (PERSONAL.XLSB) list there will be two folders: one for Microsoft Excel Objects and one for Modules. The Modules folder is the one we're interested in. Double-click that to open it, and there will be at least one Module called Module1. This should be where your newly-recorded module is residing. (If you have more than one module displayed in your Personal.xlsb file, then it's possible that other macros have been recorded before, in which case your new macro will probably be listed in the highest-numbered module).

Once you locate your macro, you should see coding very similar to this:

```
Sub PrepareVehReport()
'
' PrepareVehReport Macro

    Range("L1").Select
    ActiveCell.FormulaR1C1 = "Days In Inv"
    Range("L1").Select
Selection.Font.Bold = True
    Range("L2").Select
    ActiveCell.FormulaR1C1 = "=NOW() - RC[-1]"
    Range("L2").Select
ActiveCell.NumberFormat = "0"
Selection.Copy
ActiveCell.Offset(1, 0).Range("A1").Select
ActiveSheet.Paste

End Sub
```

Side Point

Right above the "Sub PrepareVehReport()" line, you may see
the line "Option Explicit". This line becomes increasingly
important the more you work with macros. It's a statement that
forces Excel to examine your code and look for inconsistencies in
any variables you create in your program. You'll learn more about
variables in these case studies. If you don't see that line at the top
of the code window, you can always type it in manually. You can
also make Excel enter this line automatically in your code
modules, but for our basic examples in these case studies, it's not
strictly necessary to have this line.

If you examine the coding, you'll pretty quickly be able
to see how the recorder writes its own code based on
what you do. For example, you selected cell L1. You
entered "Days In Inv". You re-selected that cell and

made it bold. All these instructions are what you can see in the first few lines.

This gives us the beginning of our macro. What we want to do, however, is modify it to make it work on its own, and fill in ALL the days in inventory for all the cars in the spreadsheet.

So we're going to learn a few simple concepts about Excel programming by manually modifying this code. First of all, the first few lines of code are fine. We don't need to touch those, because we always want Excel to go to cell L1, enter the "Days In Inv" text, make it bold, and create the first formula. We are, however, going to break into the code partway down and make some changes.

Just below the line:

```
ActiveCell.Offset(1, 0).Range("A1").Select
```

Press Enter a few times to open up some space. This is where we build some "smarts" into the macro. We want Excel to automatically copy this formula down for as many vehicles as there are in the spreadsheet. To do that, we create a simple loop. Just above the formula line:

```
ActiveSheet.Paste
```

Type this line:

```
Do Until ActiveCell.Offset(0, -1).Value = ""
```

What does this line mean? One of the simplest ways to create a loop in programming is with what's called the Do Until loop. This does *something* until *something* happens. In this case we want Excel to do the something until the entry date field is blank, in which case we've run out of cars in the spreadsheet (assuming all your cars have entry dates. They do, don't they?)

In Excel you can refer to any cell in the spreadsheet in relation to where the current active cell is. To do that you use what's called an Offset, which tells Excel where you want to look in relation to where the current cell is. You need to supply the row and column of the offset, which is what you see in the numbers after the word Offset. So this statement is saying: I want you to do something until the cell zero rows from my current location and -1 columns from my current location equals "" (in other words, is blank. No entry date.)

Hang in there, folks, you'll see how this all comes together pretty quickly. Now, what is it that we want Excel to do in this loop? We want to copy that formula down for as many cars as there are. Inside our loop, our first instruction is to copy the formula:

```
ActiveSheet.Paste
```

Now move your cursor up in the code to the line:

```
ActiveCell.Offset(1, 0).Range("A1").Select
```

Highlight this entire line and press Ctrl-C to copy it. Move your cursor back down to just below our `ActiveSheet.Paste`line,and press Ctrl-V to paste it. That line of code tells Excel to move the cursor down one cell relative to where it is now.

At this point, here's pretty much what your modified macro should look like:

```
Sub PrepareVehReport()
'
' PrepareVehReport Macro

    Range("L1").Select
    ActiveCell.FormulaR1C1 = "Days In Inv"
    Range("L1").Select
Selection.Font.Bold = True
    Range("L2").Select
    ActiveCell.FormulaR1C1 = "=NOW() - RC[-1]"
    Range("L2").Select
ActiveCell.NumberFormat = "0"
Selection.Copy
ActiveCell.Offset(1, 0).Range("A1").Select
        Do Until ActiveCell.Offset(0, -1).Value = ""
        ActiveSheet.Paste
ActiveCell.Offset(1, 0).Range("A1").Select

End Sub
```

Okay, we're almost done with our loop. So far we're saying, "Do the following steps until the cell to the left of my current location is blank:

1. Paste the formula into the cell

2. Move down one cell

Pretty simple, huh? All we need to do now is close the loop. We need a statement that makes Excel go back to the beginning of the loop and check again to see if the cell to the left of its current location is blank. Here it is:

```
Loop
```

Yep, it's that simple. After Excel executes the two statements inside the loop, it hits this line and knows to go back up to the Do Until line to see if that statement is still true. Let's add two more lines of code to finish the macro. Below the Loop line, enter:

```
Application.CutCopyMode = False
    Range("A1").Select
```

These two lines of code simply take Excel out of copy-paste mode and then selects cell A1 to take us back to the home cell.

Here's what our code should look like now:

```
Sub PrepareVehReport()
'
' PrepareVehReport Macro

    Range("L1").Select
    ActiveCell.FormulaR1C1 = "Days In Inv"
    Range("L1").Select
Selection.Font.Bold = True
    Range("L2").Select
    ActiveCell.FormulaR1C1 = "=NOW() - RC[-1]"
```

```
    Range("L2").Select
ActiveCell.NumberFormat = "0"
Selection.Copy
ActiveCell.Offset(1, 0).Range("A1").Select

   Do Until ActiveCell.Offset(0, -1).Value = ""
ActiveSheet.Paste
ActiveCell.Offset(1, 0).Range("A1").Select
   Loop

Application.CutCopyMode = False
   Range("A1").Select
End Sub
```

After Excel does this operation over and over, entering the formula, moving down one cell, checking the cell to its left to see if it's blank, eventually it WILL be blank. There will be no more cars in the spreadsheet. So the loop is finished and Excel moves on to whatever is next in the macro, which, in this case, is nothing. The End Sub line finished the macro.

Let's see how our macro does. Back in Excel, on the Developer tab, then Macros. Find the PrepareVehReport macro, select it if necessary, and click Run. If the macro is modified correctly, you should see Excel type the "Days In Inv" header in L1, enter the formula in cell L2, and paste the formula down for as many cars as there are in the report. This will happen in very short order, probably less than a second or two. If something goes wrong, you will get an error message, and you'll have to review your code to see where it differs from the lines in the example above.

Congratulations! Step 1 of our workbook is done. But we're not done yet. We still need to create our subtotals in the report and format it for printing. So to do that, we're going to create two more macros.

Side point

Problems? If something goes wrong with your macro, most of the time any changes made to the workbook are irreversible. In this case, simply close the workbook and don't save changes. When you reopen it, everything will be back as it was before the macro ran. In the case where you are storing the macro in the workbook instead of your personal.xlsb file, make sure you save the workbook BEFORE you run the macro. That way, any changes made to the workbook will be undone, but your code will still be intact. (Don't worry, after you *forget* to save the workbook prior to running your macro and running into problems a few times, two things will probably happen: 1: you'll curse like a drunken sailor, and 2: you'll start to remember to save your workbook prior to running your macro.)

Side point

If you start writing macros, I guarantee this will happen to you sooner or later: you'll start the macro, and everything freezes up. Maybe you'll get a flickering screen, maybe the display will turn white, maybe the computer slows down to a sickening crawl. What happened? Sometimes you outsmart yourself and write a portion of your macro that gets stuck in a never-ending loop. Perhaps you forgot to tell your macro to move down a cell after doing something, or perhaps you forgot to tell your macro to check for a changing condition in the spreadsheet. If this happens, your macro will happily chug along, sucking up every bit of available resources in your computer. If it seems like your macro is taking an unusually long time or you notice one of the conditions above, generally you can press the Ctrl-Pause/Break keys together, and Excel will break into the macro and stop it. Generally. After that, you can examine your code to see where you went wrong. If the Ctrl-Break option doesn't stop the macro, however, you're usually stuck with the old Ctrl-Alt-Delete option, going to Task Manager and stopping Excel.

Because the data is already sorted the way we need it, we don't need to have Excel do that for us. So we can start by creating the subtotals, which will give us our report breaks.

Once again, let's fire up our macro recorder by clicking the Developer tab, then Record Macro. Let's name this one something like "CreateSubtotals" and make sure we're storing it in personal.xlsb. Now the recorder is recording. Make sure Use Relative Reference button is still clicked (depressed). Then press Control-Home to automatically move your cursor to cell A1. Now the first thing we want to do is create our report breaks. Because we need to make sure we're applying these breaks to our entire spreadsheet data range, we need to select this entire range by pressing Ctrl-Shift-* (Hold down the Ctrl and Shift keys and then the 8 on the numbers key row). When you do, Excel automatically highlights the entire data range. We're ready to start our report breaks.

Click the Data tab, then Subtotals. We're going to create report breaks on two different levels. The major break will be on make, followed by model. To do this, we create our first subtotal, then go back and do our second subtotal.

Click the "At each change in:" dropdown box and select Make. Click the "Use function:" dropdown box and select Count. Finally, in the "Add subtotal to:" list, select Make. Then click OK.

You'll see Excel crank through the spreadsheet and add a subtotal line below each change in vehicle make. Now, the next thing we want to do is press Ctrl-Home again, then Ctrl-Shift 8 again. Why? Because we're going to create our second report break, and Excel has the necessary range already highlighted for us. (Technically, Excel has already selected the correct range for us to create the second subtotal, but this ensures that we always have the correct range before creating the second subtotal).

Click the Data tab again, then Subtotal. This time we will select Model from the first dropdown. Leave Count in the second, but in the "Add subtotal list to:" list, uncheck Make and check Model. Now, THIS IS ALSO IMPORTANT: In the Replace Current Subtotals line, uncheck that box. The reason for this is because we want to leave the current Make subtotals in place and simply add a new subtotal for Model.

After you click OK, you'll now see a break for every new model and also one for every new make. Now the salespeople will know how many makes and models we have in inventory.

One final step for this macro. Click the top of column A to select the entire column, then drag your mouse across to select columns A through L. At the very end of column L, double-click your mouse when the cursor turns to a double-headed arrow. This will widen all the selected columns to their widest needed width. Then click back to A1.

Stop the macro recorder by clicking the Developer tab, then click Stop Recording. Press Alt-F11 to fire up the VBA editor. You should now see a macro that looks very similar to this:

```
Sub CreateSubtotals()
'
' CreateSubtotals Macro
'

'
Selection.CurrentRegion.Select
Selection.SubtotalGroupBy:=3, Function:=xlCount, TotalList:=Array(3), _
    Replace:=True, PageBreaks:=False, SummaryBelowData:=True
  Range("A1").Select
Selection.CurrentRegion.Select
Selection.SubtotalGroupBy:=4, Function:=xlCount, TotalList:=Array(4), _
    Replace:=False, PageBreaks:=False, SummaryBelowData:=True
ActiveCell.Columns("A:L").EntireColumn.Select
ActiveCell.Columns("A:L").EntireColumn.EntireColumn.AutoFit
ActiveCell.Select
End Sub
```

We won't spend much time trying to delve into this, but if you examine it for a few minutes you'll see that it's not too difficult to interpret. You can see the two subtotal operations you performed, one by make and one by model. In the first subtotal you chose to replace any current subtotals (Replace:=True), but in the second subtotal you chose not to replace any existing subtotals (Replace:=False). By examining the code Excel writes in this way, you can begin to learn quite a lot just by observation.

The last step is to format the page for printing. If we were simply to print this spreadsheet as it is, we would get a messy report. Excel will automatically spill the additional columns across multiple pages. We, on the other hand, want all the columns to fit on one page. We don't care how many pages of vehicles the report prints, but we only want it to be one page wide.

So we need to record one more macro. Once again, start the macro recorder. Let's call this one FormatReport. When the recorder is running, click the File tab, then Print. On the Print screen, click the No Scaling dropdown and select Fit All Columns on One Page. Exit the Print screen by clicking the back arrow at the top. On the Page Layout tab, click the Print Titles button. Click in the "Rows to repeat at top:" field, then click the "1" in row one of your Excel spreadsheet. This will make "$1:$1" appear in the Rows to repeat at top field.

Then click OK to close the dialog box.

Now you can stop the recorder. If you click the Print Preview button on your toolbar, you'll see that the report will be 1 page wide by however many tall it needs to be.

Super Excel for Dealership Management

Once again, press Alt-F11 to go to the VBA editor. Look for your FormatReport macro. Now, this may come as a bit of a shock, because Excel is VERY verbose when it comes to this, creating a line of code for every possible print setting. A lot of these lines could be removed manually, since Excel will use its default settings anyway. But you can leave all these lines in there since it doesn't hurt anything. Depending on your version of Excel, you'll probably see something resembling this:

```
Sub FormatReport()
'
' FormatReport Macro
Application.PrintCommunication = False
    With ActiveSheet.PageSetup
       .PrintTitleRows = ""
       .PrintTitleColumns = ""
    End With
Application.PrintCommunication = True
ActiveSheet.PageSetup.PrintArea = ""
Application.PrintCommunication = False
    With ActiveSheet.PageSetup
       .LeftHeader = ""
       .CenterHeader = ""
       .RightHeader = ""
       .LeftFooter = ""
       .CenterFooter = ""
       .RightFooter = ""
       .LeftMargin = Application.InchesToPoints(0.7)
       .RightMargin = Application.InchesToPoints(0.7)
       .TopMargin = Application.InchesToPoints(0.75)
       .BottomMargin = Application.InchesToPoints(0.75)
       .HeaderMargin = Application.InchesToPoints(0.3)
       .FooterMargin = Application.InchesToPoints(0.3)
       .PrintHeadings = False
       .PrintGridlines = False
       .PrintComments = xlPrintNoComments
       .CenterHorizontally = False
```

```
        .CenterVertically = False
        .Orientation = xlPortrait
        .Draft = False
        .PaperSize = xlPaperLetter
        .FirstPageNumber = xlAutomatic
        .Order = xlDownThenOver
        .BlackAndWhite = False
```

...and on and on. Yikes. Thank goodness we don't have to type any of THIS stuff manually.

Now we're ready to put it all together. Remember, we have 3 macros we've just recorded and modified. We could run through the macros one at a time every time we want a new report, but because we want to automate this as much as possible, let's make Excel do that for us.

If you locate our first macro, PrepareVehReport, you'll see that it ends with Range("A1").Select just after our Do Until loop. After Excel copies our formula down the line, the loop stops and the macro ends. Let's modify that to make it run our other two macros. Just above the End Sub line, press Enter a few times to open some space. Just above the End Sub line, type:

```
CreateSubtotals
FormatReport
Msgbox("Report preparation complete")
```

When you're done, your macro should look something like this:

```
Sub PrepareVehReport()
'
```

```
' PrepareVehReport Macro


    Range("L1").Select
    ActiveCell.FormulaR1C1 = "Days In Inv"
    Range("L1").Select
Selection.Font.Bold = True
    Range("L2").Select
    ActiveCell.FormulaR1C1 = "=NOW() - RC[-1]"
    Range("L2").Select
ActiveCell.NumberFormat = "0"
Selection.Copy
ActiveCell.Offset(1, 0).Range("A1").Select


    Do Until ActiveCell.Offset(0, -1).Value = ""
        ActiveSheet.Paste
        ActiveCell.Offset(1, 0).Range("A1").Select
Loop


Create_Subtotals
Format_Report
Msgbox("Report preparation complete")
End Sub
```

The lines CreateSubtotals and FormatReport, as you remember, are the names of our other two macros. VBA allows you to call other macros from within a macro. So our instructions for our PrepareVehReport are carried out first, then VBA calls the CreateSubtotals macro to run. After that macro finished, the next instruction is to call our FormatReport macro. After that finishes, we have a simple message box that pops up and tells us our report is ready to print.

Now let's see if it all works. Close Excel without saving any changes to the car_inv_before.xlsx workbook, but save the personal.xlsb file when prompted. Re-open your car_inv_before.xlsx workbook, then click the Developer tab, Macros, and selecting the PrepareVehReport macro. When you click Run, you should see the Days In Inv column populated, the subtotals automatically entered, and maybe a flicker or two while the formatting is set for printing. Finally, you'll see your message box:

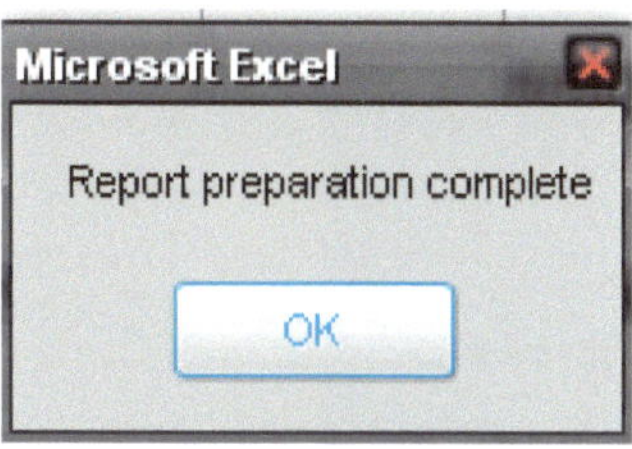

If things don't work correctly, you can review your code for differences from the above coding, or you can open the car_inv_after.xlsm file, which contains the coding in the workbook itself. You can open it and run the PrepareVehReport macro, and see how the code creates the final report.

So there you have it. A simple spreadsheet that can now be modified and prepared for printing at the click of a button. Keep in mind that this macro is designed only for this particular spreadsheet, but the concepts apply to any spreadsheet. By following these steps of recording your macro, you can make Excel repeat those steps every time, saving YOU a lot of time and getting the results everybody wants.

Case Study #2 - Building flexible workbooks

"If you put water into a cup, it becomes the cup. You put water into a bottle and it becomes the bottle. You put it in a teapot it becomes the teapot. Now, water can flow or it can crash. Be water, my friend."
- Bruce Lee

Example 1: Gross_Book.xls

For our next case study, we'll be building a spreadsheet that lets the viewer see the performance of each salesperson in the dealership. The spreadsheet will list the salesperson name, percent of front-end gross, number of vehicles sold, total front-end gross amount, and average gross per unit.

But that in itself would only be a "standard" manual spreadsheet. We want automation. And we want flexibility. We want our workbook to be the water that flows, as Bruce Lee said. What if the manager or GM wanted to see that list sorted by total front-end gross? Or average front-end gross? Or number of vehicles sold? Or switch back and forth between any of the three choices?

So we're going to add a little something: a set of option buttons that allows the user to view the list by any of those criteria.

First off, where do we get the data? This typically comes from some form of standard gross book report available on the DMS, or it may be something you can create and download as an Excel or text file. Since we're dealing more with the Excel side in this section than the DMS side, we won't get into the nitty-gritty of the source data.

Our workbook will consist of two worksheets: the data sheet and the analysis sheet. The analysis sheet will use a series of formulas to examine the data sheet and display the results. First let's look at the data sheet:

Super Excel for Dealership Management

	A	B	C	D	E	F	G	H
1				**Gross Book Report**				
2								
3	**Salesperson**	**ID**	**Deal**	**Sold**	**Buyer**	**StkNo**	**Yr / Model**	**Front-End**
4	HOUSE	101	48986	5/1/2024	PETRUZIELL		05 LS430	0
5	HOUSE	101	48997	5/2/2024	MAGANA,JOH	100134A	04 RX330	0
6	HESTON,CHARLTON	7676	49071	5/7/2024	APOLONIO,D	18417P	06 ES330	0
7	HESTON,CHARLTON	7676	49073	5/7/2024	YORK JR,WA	100041	10 RX350	1,352
8	HESTON,CHARLTON	7676	49082	5/7/2024	KHAN,URSZU	18403P	06 GS300	3,549
9	HESTON,CHARLTON	7676	49086	5/7/2024	ELLESIN,JU	18418P	06 ES330	0
10	HESTON,CHARLTON	7676	49109	5/9/2024	KRIEGER,LA	90863A	04 SC430	2,688
11	BALDWIN,ADAM	7746	47771	5/5/2024	WEST,ROBER	100144T	10 RX350	2,267
12	NEWMAN,PAUL	7753	49070	5/6/2024	KOURY,DENN	18336P	06 RX330	184
13	NEWMAN,PAUL	7753	49092	5/8/2024	BEHARRY,TH	18394PA	01 4RUN	3,750
14	FIELDS,SALLY	7775	49063	5/6/2024	VEERAPPAN,	18405P	07 RX350	3,195
15	FIELDS,SALLY	7775	49080	5/7/2024	HAMILTON,T	100155T	10 RX350	660
16	REDFORD,ROBERT	7839	49038	5/7/2024	GENTILE,AL	90750	09 IS250	992
17	REDFORD,ROBERT	7839	49043	5/11/2024	GREEN,ROE	100072	10 RX350	3,233
18	OLDMAN,GARY	7840	49058	5/6/2024	ANDERSON,E	100125T	10 RX350	2,178
19	OLDMAN,GARY	7840	49102	5/9/2024	HORNE,GINA	91035	09 ES350	409
20	RABBIT,ROGER	8552	49075	5/7/2024	NIXON,VICT	91034	09 ES350	1,312
21	RABBIT,ROGER	8552	49050	5/7/2024	DIGERONIMO	100150T	10 RX350	2,001
22	RABBIT,ROGER	8552	49097	5/9/2024	CO,DENNIS	82668	08 RX400	409
23	HEMINGWAY,MURIEL	9210	49022	5/4/2024	HAGGERTY,C	18366PA	04 TOWNC	947
24	HEMINGWAY,MURIEL	9210	49041	5/4/2024	BARRETT,MA	18365P	06 ES330	300
25	HEMINGWAY,MURIEL	9210	49090	5/7/2024	SCHUETZ,CH	18326P	06 4RUN	758
26	HEMINGWAY,MURIEL	9210	49101	5/9/2024	MUSCH,SHAR	18318P	07 C280	1,025
27	HURT,WILLIAM	9219	48992	5/8/2024	DCI MANAGE	100145T	10 RX350	2,344
28	BAIO,SCOTT	9536	49112	5/9/2024	CHAWLA,YUG	18383P	05 LS430	2,462
29	HANKS,TOM	16	49096	5/9/2024	COLA,PHILI	100133	10 RX350	1,816
30	BLACK,JACK	272	49067	5/6/2024	AXNER,GARY	90649	09 IS250	1,692
31	BALE,CHRISTIAN	272	49069	5/6/2024	LISCOE,HIL	100154T	10 RX350	1,566
32	DOWNEY,ROBERT JR.	709	49077	5/7/2024	MOLNAR,CHR	90994TA	03 DEVI	314

We have columns for the salesperson name and ID, deal number, sold date, buyer name, stock number, year and model, and front-end amount. Much of this information is not contained in the analysis page, but we capture it so that if there is a dispute on a salesperson's amount or ranking, the user has only to click on the data sheet to see all the details.

Now let's look at the analysis sheet:

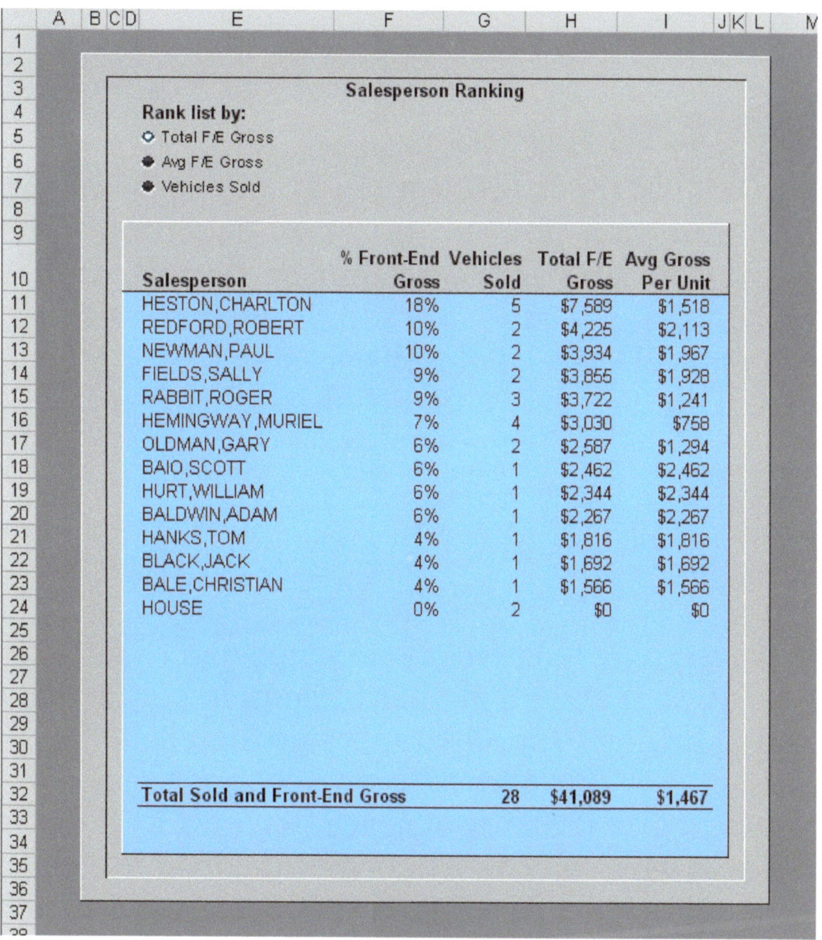

Salesperson Ranking

Rank list by:
- ○ Total F/E Gross
- ● Avg F/E Gross
- ● Vehicles Sold

Salesperson	% Front-End Gross	Vehicles Sold	Total F/E Gross	Avg Gross Per Unit
HESTON,CHARLTON	18%	5	$7,589	$1,518
REDFORD,ROBERT	10%	2	$4,225	$2,113
NEWMAN,PAUL	10%	2	$3,934	$1,967
FIELDS,SALLY	9%	2	$3,855	$1,928
RABBIT,ROGER	9%	3	$3,722	$1,241
HEMINGWAY,MURIEL	7%	4	$3,030	$758
OLDMAN,GARY	6%	2	$2,587	$1,294
BAIO,SCOTT	6%	1	$2,462	$2,462
HURT,WILLIAM	6%	1	$2,344	$2,344
BALDWIN,ADAM	6%	1	$2,267	$2,267
HANKS,TOM	4%	1	$1,816	$1,816
BLACK,JACK	4%	1	$1,692	$1,692
BALE,CHRISTIAN	4%	1	$1,566	$1,566
HOUSE	0%	2	$0	$0
Total Sold and Front-End Gross		28	$41,089	$1,467

We've dressed this one up a bit for looks, but we'll be creating a fairly unadorned one just to show the functionality.

Step 1: Foundation

First let's build the data sheet. In a new workbook (or you can simply open the gross_book_stage1.xlsx file if you want to see the first stage already completed), Name the worksheet as "Data", and add the columns for Salesperson, ID, Deal, Sold, Buyer, StkNo, Yr / Model, and Front-End as shown in the illustration.

	A	B	C	D	E	F	G	H
1								
2								
3	Salesperson	ID	Deal	Sold	Buyer	StkNo	Yr / Model	Front-End

Next, we're going to create some range names for our data sheet, so that we can refer to them in our formulas instead of having to specify ranges by their cell addresses. For this particular one I chose a range of 300 rows to give it plenty of space (technically 296, since I'm starting on row 4). If your dealership sells more than 300 cars per month, then you should decide on your range accordingly. With your cursor in cell A4 (or just below the Salesperson header if your row starts differently), hold down the Shift key, tap your right-arrow on the keyboard, and go to column H, the last column. When you get there, while still holding down the Shift key, press the Page Down button until you get to row 300, or however far down you want to go for the maximum potential number of cars you think you'll sell in a given month. Now you can let go of the Shift key.

Click the Formulas tab, then Define Name. The Define Name dialog box will appear. In the top box type DataTable (no spaces).

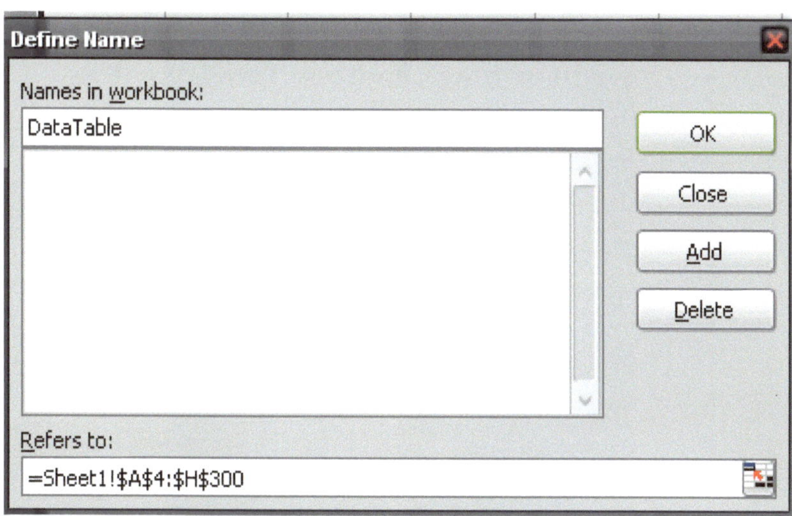

You can see that this name applies to the range you have selected. Click OK. If you want, you can format the cells in that range to a different color, as we have in the final workbook, so that you have a visual indicator of the range.

Next we'll create a range for the salespeople. With your cursor in A4 again, hold down the shift key and press Page Down until you get to the bottom of your selected row (300 or whatever you chose earlier). Just as above, define a new range name and call it SalesPeopleList.

Finally, we'll create a range for the front-end numbers. With your cursor in H4 (if that's the column that contains your front-end numbers), hold down the shift key and press Page Down to the bottom of your selected range. Define a new range called FrontEndList.

That will take care of our Data sheet. Using these range names, we can easily refer to them anywhere in the workbook.

Side Point

Want to know where a range in the workbook applies to? Press F5 to bring up the GoTo dialog box, then select the assigned range name in the list box. When you press Enter, Excel will take you to that range in the workbook and highlight it for you.

Now for our Analysis page. Add a new page to the workbook if necessary and name it Analysis. You can build a fancy portion of this sheet to hold the salespeople information, with different colors, highlighted borders, and so on, like we have in the final workbook, but it's not necessary. On this page we start out by adding our columns for Salesperson, % of Front-End Gross, Vehicles Sold, Total Front-End Gross, and Avg Gross per Unit. Create these column headers around row 10 or so, in order to leave room later for the option buttons we'll be adding.

Leave enough rows open for the number of salespeople you have in your dealership, plus some room for growth. Just below that, type Total Sold and Front-End Gross.

	A	B	C	D	E	F	G	H	I
						% Front-End Gross	Vehicles Sold	Total F/E Gross	Avg Gross Per Unit
10					Salesperson				
32					Total Sold and Front-End Gross				

In the "Total Sold and Front-End Gross" row just under the Vehicles Sold column, enter a SUM formula for the number of rows from your header row (e.g. =SUM(G11:G31)). Copy and paste that formula to the Total Front-End Gross column. In the Avg Gross Per Unit column in that row, type a division function that divides the total gross by the number of vehicles sold. Remember that you'll get an error if you try to divide by zero, so you can account for that in your formula. For example, here's the formula used in the sample spreadsheet:

```
=IF(G32<>0,H32/G32,0)
```

Our totals row is 32, so the formula says, in effect, If G32 is not equal to 0, then divide H32 by G32, otherwise return a zero.

Now we're going to create another range. Highlight the area just below the header row, from Salesperson to Avg Gross Per Unit, down to just above your total line. Again, click Insert, Range, Name, and type AnalysisTable as the name. Click OK.

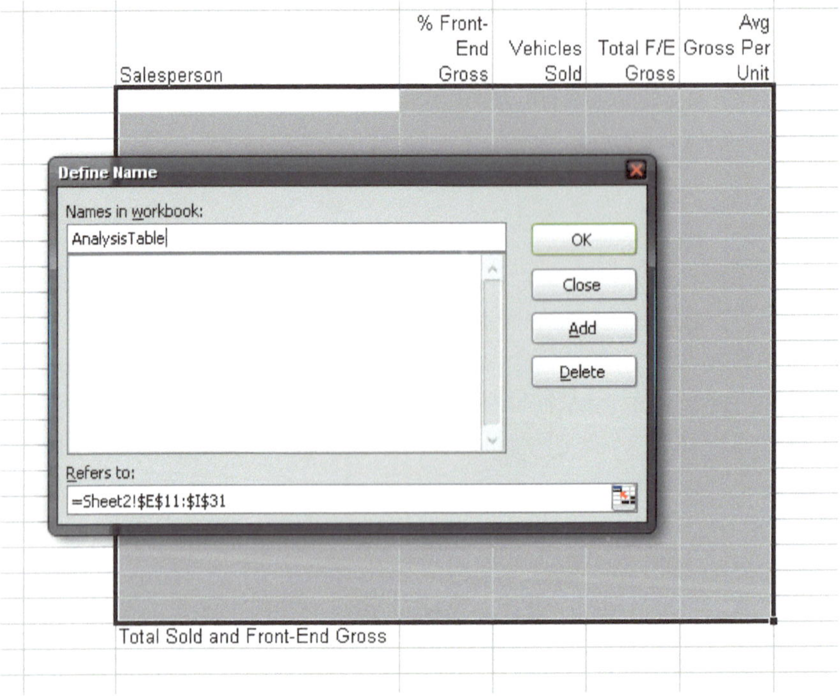

With your cursor in the total row in the Total Front-End Gross column, insert a range and call it TotalGross.

Now that all of our range names are created and totals formulas are ready, we can work on the formulas for the analysis range. Just below the % of Front-End Gross header, type the formula:

```
=IF(TotalGross<> 0,SUMIF(SalespeopleList,E11,FrontEndList)/TotalGross,0)
```

(this is assuming your starting column for the analysis range is E, and your row for the analysis range is 11).

Let's take a look at that formula to understand what it's saying. This is a standard SUMIF formula, and because we've created our range names, it's a lot easier to understand than the more cryptic cell names. So our formula is saying, in effect:

"Wherever, in the SalespeopleList, there's a match to whatever is in E11, sum the numbers in the FrontEndList range for that name. Then divide that total number by the number that's in the TotalGross range."

Remember our SalespeopleList range is the range of all the salespeople in our Data page, and the FrontEndList range is the range of all the front-end numbers. So the SUMIF function finds every match to a given salesperson, and for every match, adds the corresponding front-end gross number to its total. Then it simply divides that total by whatever the number is in the Front-End Gross total.

Next is our Vehicles Sold column. Just under the header, type:

```
=COUNTIF(SalesPeopleList,E11)
```

In this formula, we're simply counting the number of times the salesperson's name shows up in the Data range. Every time it finds a match, that's another car sold.

Next, our Total Front-End Gross column. Just under the header, type:

```
=SUMIF(SalesPeopleList,E11,FrontEndList)
```

This may look familiar. It is, in fact, a simpler version of our first formula, only without the division, which means that this formula is adding up all the front-end numbers where there's a match to the salesperson.

Finally, under the Avg Gross Per Unit header, simply go down to the total row and copy and paste that formula into I11. Since that formula always divides the total front-end gross by the number of cars sold, it's the same formula regardless of what line it's on.

Now that your first row of formulas is entered, simply copy and paste all the formulas in that row down to just above the total line.

You could further prepare your Analysis section by entering the current salespeople you have in your dealership. But this part is important: the names must be entered exactly as they appear on the Data page. That's how the formulas in the Analysis range work, by looking up the corresponding names and returning the total front-end gross numbers.

Your spreadsheet is now ready to accept information from the Data sheet. Once the information is put in, either through an Excel macro that pulls the data from a print file, or through copying and pasting from a downloaded file from the DMS, the Analysis page will update automatically once the salespeople are entered in the Analysis page. The only other thing necessary will be to verify that the salesperson names are entered exactly as shown in the Data page.

Step 2: Flexibility

In our first example, gross_book_stage1.xls, we built the workbook, attempting to do so with a good foundation. We separated our data page from the analysis page; we created named ranges for easy reference, and created formulas that are efficient and powerful. Now we want to add some flexibility to the workbook.

We'll be starting with gross_book_stage2.xls. This is essentially the same as the stage 1 workbook but has been formatted for presentation. We're now going to add some controls and coding to the workbook that will allow the user to view the salesperson list by 3 different ranking levels: Total Front-End Gross, Average Front-End Gross, and number of vehicles sold. The user will see a set of option buttons and can re-sort the salesperson list by any of these three choices.

First let's open gross_book_stage2.xls. The Data page has data in it, and the Analysis page is populated with its information. Notice the blank area under the heading "Rank list by:". This is where we'll be adding our option buttons.

On the Developer tab, click the Insert dropdown. You'll see a set of icons that represent controls you can add to your worksheet.

In the ActiveX Controls region, click your mouse on the Option Button tool, then move the mouse to the area just below the "Rank list by:" header. Click the mouse once, and a default option button will appear. Click again on the option button icon on the toolbar, then click your mouse just below the option button you just added. Then again, so that there are 3 option buttons stacked on top of each other, something like this:

OptionButton1
OptionButton2
OptionButton3

Next, right-click on OptionButton1 and choose Properties. The Properties window will appear for this control. Change the Name to "optTotalGross", the Caption to "Total F/E Gross", and under GroupName type "Salesperson". Click the BackColor row, and a drop-down box will appear. Choose the gray cell in the 3rd row down so that the background color matches the spreadsheet color. Then click the x to close the Properties window.

Side point

Notice that when you began adding the option buttons to your worksheet, the Design Mode button changed to a "pressed down" look. This was to show that you are in Design Mode while adding and working with controls. While you're in Design Mode, you can do anything you need to in order to set their location, properties, etc. Once you're done working with your controls, you can click the Design Mode button to take you out of Design Mode, and your controls are now truly functional on the worksheet.

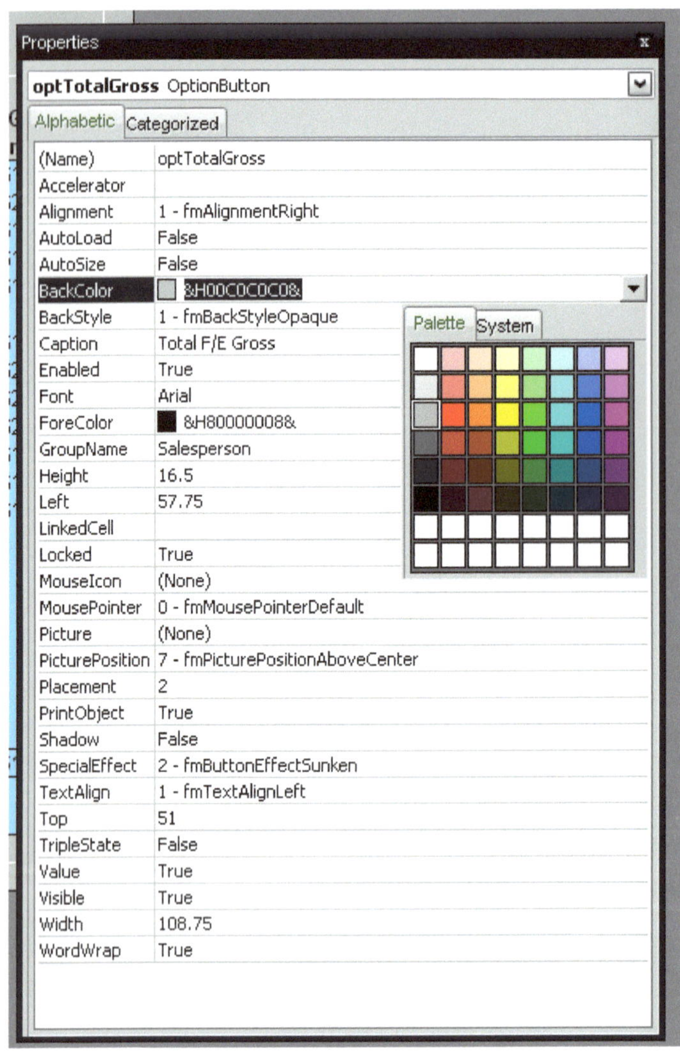

Do this same operation for the other two option buttons. On the second button, the name will be optAvgGross, caption will be Avg F/E Gross, and the group

Salesperson. The third option button's name will be optCarsSold, caption will be Vehicles Sold, and again, group will be Salesperson. When we're done, we have something that looks similar to this:

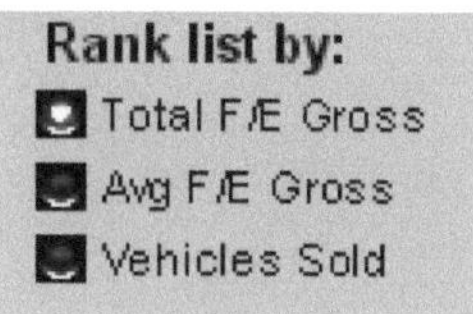

Side point

You'll notice we entered Salesperson for all 3 groups in these controls. A group for controls (particularly for option buttons) is a way to segregate different controls for different groups. If, for example, we had another set of 3 option buttons on this spreadsheet for a different purpose, we would enter a different name for that group. The purpose of the group is so that the options are available only in that group; the choices are mutually exclusive. The choices for Salesperson group only apply to that group. The choices for another group would apply only to that group. In this case, since there's only one group, it's really not necessary to add them to a group called Salesperson. But we do it anyway for good design. If we ever needed to add another set of buttons for something else, we already have our Salesperson group segregated.

Now let's add the code that will sort our salesperson list by the 3 different criteria. On the Developer tab, click Record Macro. We're going to call it "SortByTotalGross", and we're going to save it in This Workbook:

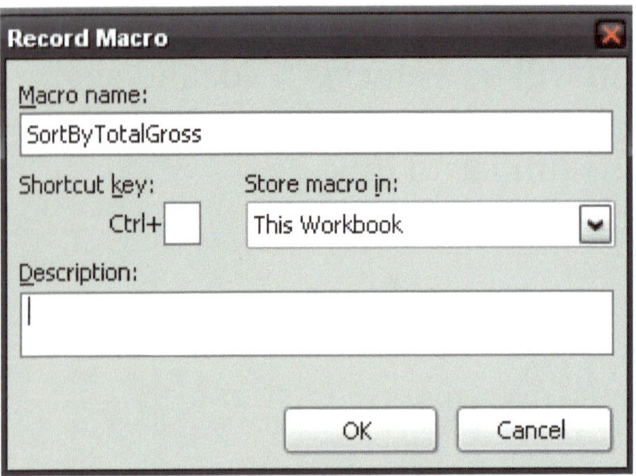

When you click OK, you'll be in record mode. Press F5 to bring up the GoTo window, and choose AnalysisTable (remember that? Here's one of the reasons name ranges come in handy!)

When the AnalysisTable range is highlighted, click Data, then Sort. For the first Sort by option, choose Total F/E Gross. For the second choice, choose Salesperson. Then click OK.

The list will sort by your chosen criteria. Click your mouse in cell A1 to deselect the AnalysisTable range. Stop the Macro recorder by clicking the Stop button.

Press Alt-F11 to bring up the VBA editor, then locate the macro you just wrote, probably under Module 1 in the gross_book_stage2.xlsx spreadsheet:

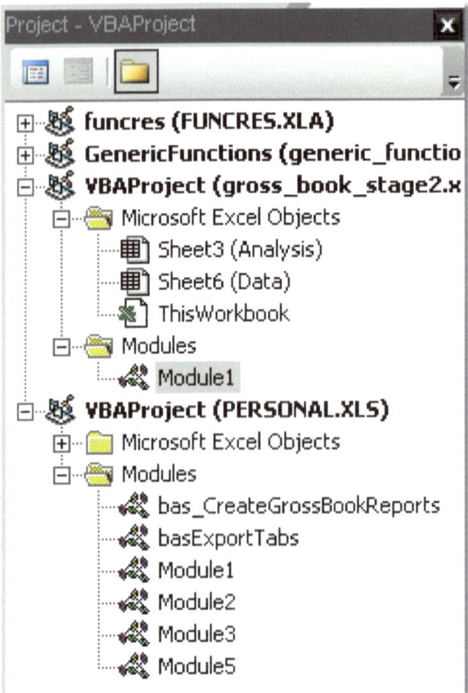

Your macro should look very similar to this:

```
Sub SortByTotalGross()
'
' SortByTotalGross Macro
' Sort lists by Total F/E Gross
'
    Range("AnalysisTable").Select
Selection.Sort Key1:=Range("H11"), Order1:=xlDescending, Key2:=Range("E11") _
    , Order2:=xlAscending, Header:=xlGuess, OrderCustom:=1, MatchCase:= _
    False, Orientation:=xlTopToBottom, DataOption1:=xlSortNormal, DataOption2 _
    :=xlSortNormal
    Range("A1").Select
End Sub
```

We're going to manually add two more lines to this code. Just above the line:

```
Range("AnalysisTable").Select
```

Add the line:

```
Application.ScreenUpdating = False
```

And just above the End Sub line, add the line:

```
Application.ScreenUpdating = True
```

These two commands turn off and turn on screen updating. These aren't necessary in order for the macro to work, but you'll find yourself using them the more you write macros. These commands serve two purposes: they turn off that annoying screen flicker when a macro is doing something (like sorting records), and they speed up the macro. Without the screen having to update while the macro is running, it saves a significant amount of processor time.

Now let's add our next sort routine. Back in Excel, fire up the macro recorder. Let's call this one SortByAvgGross, save it, again, in this workbook, and start recording. Select our AnalysisTable range, click Data, Sort, then sort first by Avg Gross Per Unit, then by Salesperson. Select cell A1, then stop the macro recorder.

Finally, one more macro. Same routine, only this time we'll call it SortByCarsSold. Once the recorder is running, select your range, sort first by Vehicles Sold, then Salesperson. Select cell A1, then stop the recorder.

Back in our VBA editor, we can now see all three sort routines. Let's add our Application.ScreenUpdating statements to these last two, the same as we did with our first one. Our SortByAvgGross macro should look similar to this:

```
Sub SortByAvgGross()
'
' SortByAvgGross Macro
' Sort lists by Avg F/E Gross
'
Application.ScreenUpdating = False
    Range("AnalysisTable").Select
Selection.Sort Key1:=Range("I11"), Order1:=xlDescending, Key2:=Range("E11") _
    , Order2:=xlAscending, Header:=xlGuess, OrderCustom:=1, MatchCase:= _
    False, Orientation:=xlTopToBottom, DataOption1:=xlSortNormal, DataOption2 _
    :=xlSortNormal
    Range("A1").Select
Application.ScreenUpdating = True
End Sub
```

...and our SortByCarsSold macro should look similar to this:

```
Sub SortByCarsSold()
'
' SortByCarsSold Macro
' Sort lists by number of cars sold
'
Application.ScreenUpdating = False
    Range("AnalysisTable").Select
Selection.Sort Key1:=Range("G11"), Order1:=xlDescending, Key2:=Range("E11") _
    , Order2:=xlAscending, Header:=xlGuess, OrderCustom:=1, MatchCase:= _
    False, Orientation:=xlTopToBottom, DataOption1:=xlSortNormal, DataOption2 _
    :=xlSortNormal
    Range("A1").Select
Application.ScreenUpdating = True
End Sub
```

Back to our option buttons. Let's add some code to make these guys actually do some work. On the Developer tab let's go back into Design mode by clicking the Design Mode button, then we'll start by double-clicking the Total F/E Gross button. When you do, the Excel VBA editor will open up, and the skeleton of a macro will be automatically created for you:

```
Private Sub optTotalGross_Click()

End Sub
```

Side Point

This is what's called an Event Procedure. Excel, like other programs and Windows itself, spends a lot of time doing the equivalent of twiddling its thumbs, waiting for something to happen. Actually, it's keeping track of a LOT of things. Did the user move his mouse? Did the user click in a cell? Did the user choose an option from a menu? Did the...well, you get the idea. What we've just done here is create our own event that Excel will also keep track of and will acknowledge it in the *event* that the option button is clicked. What will Excel do? Nothing. Because we haven't told the event we wanted to do anything. Once we tell it what we want to do, however, Excel will do just that when the option button is clicked.

Now, watch how easy it is to write THIS macro. Right above the End Sub line, enter this:

```
Call SortByTotalGross
```

That's our macro. Whenever the event of the user clicking that option button occurs, Excel will run this macro, which in turn calls the SortByTotalGross macro we created earlier. Easy as pie.

I bet you know what's coming next, right? Double-click the next option button for Avg F/E Gross, add the "Call SortByAvgGross" to it, and then again for the Total Gross option button with the "Call SortByTotalGross" line.

Back in Excel, click the Design Mode button to take us out of design mode. Let's take this spreadsheet for a spin. You should now be able to click any of the 3 option buttons, and the appropriate sort procedure should run. If you run into any problems, you can review the steps above, or pull up the gross_book_stage3.xlsm file, which is our final working copy, and review the code in it.

Example 2: Commission.xls

In this example we're going to be building a salesperson commission workbook. I almost hesitate to use this as an example, because it seems so many commission plans are all over the board when it comes to dealerships. But I've seen some awfully bad ones, because "whoever" in the dealership was assigned to create one was sometimes the uncomfortable Excel user mentioned in the introduction. Through no fault of their own, they were given the task and did the best they could with what they had. The result may have been a workbook that was or is laborious to maintain.

There are some common characteristics among these types of workbooks though, so we'll build one that incorporates some of these characteristics, along with keeping to our goal of creating workbooks that 1) have a good foundation, and 2) are flexible and robust.

So. What do we want our commission workbook to do? Among other things, we want it to:

- Have one page for each salesperson
    - Because the salespeople will get their own copies of their commission sheet, the workbook will need to have a template page that will become the template for each salesperson's sheet.
- Use a standard base calculation
    - Regardless of what oddball changes may happen on a particular salesperson's sheet ("Uh, yeah..." says the new car manager, "I promised him he would get $150 instead of $100 on this deal."), there is still usually a standard base from which everyone operates.
- Contain the needed information relating to the car deal
    - Stock number, customer name, make, model, deal number, etc.
- Allow for changes per salesperson
    - See point two, need we say more?

To tell you the truth, I went back and forth on the design to present in this book, because you can build some very sophisticated workbooks for this kind of application. I started out with a simple model I used for one dealership that contains one master page of all the car deals. When the commission spreadsheets are ready to be produced, an Excel macro runs through the master sheet and creates a tab for every salesperson with all their car deals included on their page. But it's a fair amount of coding, and most people reading this book are probably more interested in creating workbooks rather than writing a lot of code.

So I settled on a version that probably most dealerships use if they use Excel for commission reports: a standard template page, and one page for each salesperson. The user moves among the different tabs, entering the car deal information for each salesperson.

In the interests of building workbooks with good foundations though, our workbook will also contain a master sheet that holds our basic rules for the pay plan. This sheet will be referred to in each salesperson's sheet. That way, if a percentage or minimum amount changes, we only need to change it once on the master sheet instead of once for each salesperson's sheet.

Disclaimer:
As I stated, we could build a very sophisticated commission workbook based on your dealership's needs, but that could take a book in itself. For example, what about split deals? What about the pay plan on this make or model versus that make or model? What about this particular salesperson that, for whatever reason, also gets a commission on F&I? What about draws? The list could go on and on. But because we're tackling the concept of building workbooks with good foundations and flexibility, we're more concerned at this level with the basics. Once we have those down, then you can take your workbooks to the next level and tailor them more to your needs.

Okay, we're going to use these as our base set of rules for each salesperson:

The salesperson will make a minimum $125 commission, even on cars with 0 gross.

If the salesperson sells up to 10 new cars of Make A, he gets 15% of the gross after pack. If he sells more than 10, he gets 20%, retroactive to all the new cars of that make.

If the salesperson sells up to 7 new cars of Make B, he gets 18% of the gross after pack. If he sells more than 7, he gets 22%, retroactive to all the new cars of that make.

If the salesperson sells up to 12 used cars, he gets 20% of the gross after pack. If he sells more than 12, he gets 25%, retroactive to all the used cars.

If the salesperson sells more than 20 cars total, he gets an additional unit bonus of $500.

And in keeping with dealership management logic, the above rules can be thrown out the window for any particular car deal. And don't TELL me this kind of thing doesn't happen in your dealership! I've personally witnessed salespeople coming to their manager and talking their way into a commission on a car sale that makes mince-meat out of their pay plan. Believe me, there's no such thing as black-or-white in the dealership's front-end department; everything is a shade of gray.

First let's create our master page. This will hold the rules we've described above. Afterwards, our template page will get its information from this page.

(If you would rather see the finished workbook, you can open commission.xlsm. Otherwise, you can follow along to see how to build it yourself). In a new workbook, double-click a worksheet tab and name it Master. We'll have two columns, one for explanation and one for the corresponding numbers:

Minimum commission	125
Make A unit threshold	10
Make A comm up to threshold	15%
Make A comm above threshold	20%
Make B unit threshold	7
Make B comm up to threshold	18%
Make B comm above threshold	22%
Used unit threshold	12
Used comm up to threshold	20%
Used comm above threshold	25%
Unit Bonus threshold	20
Unit Bonus Amount	500

You can enter this information anywhere you want to in the sheet (I started with B2 and C2 in the sample workbook). After these two columns of information are entered, we're going to create range names for the numbers.

Now, one of the smart things about Excel is that when you create a range name, Excel will look for anything close by to use as its potential name. If you place your cursor in C2 (the minimum commission amount in the sample workbook) and choose Insert, Name, Define, Excel will suggest the name "Minimum_commission", because it assumes the text to the left is what you'll want to call it. Handy, huh? So let's let Excel do the work of naming the ranges for us. After you go down the line to insert the 12 range names for the 12 numbers, you should have range names called:

    Make_A_comm_above_threshold
    Make_A_comm_up_to_threshold
    Make_A_unit_threshold
    Make_B_comm_above_threshold
    Make_B_comm_up_to_threshold
    Make_B_unit_threshold
    Minimum_commission
    Unit_Bonus_Amount
    Unit_Bonus_Threshold
    Used_comm_above_threshold
    Used_comm_up_to_threshold
    Used_unit_threshold

Below these lines, let's add 2 more:

Current Period:

Export File Path:

Next to each cell, create two named ranges: Current_Period and ExportPath.

The Current Period will be used to enter the date for the pay period, and will be linked to all salesperson sheets. The Export Path will hold a file path to a folder on your computer (or network) where salesperson PDF files will be stored (more on that later).

That's it for our Master page. You can dress it up with borders and different color cells if you like, but the functional work is done.

Now...the Template page. This will be the boilerplate page that is the basis for all of our salespeople. Insert a new page if necessary, double-click the tab name and rename it "Template".

On this page, we want to hold a copy of the information that's entered on the Master page. We'll create an area we could think of a Test Table. This will be a range that will hold our minimum commission amount and our threshold percentage for cars sold.

Let's create a header area first, which will hold our salesperson name. Below that will be our test table, and below that will be our column names for the car sales information. Below is a screenshot from the sample workbook.

Salesperson		
Name		
Current Period	April 1, 2024	

Plan	Threshold	Actual	%
Minimum commission	125		
Make A unit threshold	10	2	15%
Make B unit threshold	7	1	18%
Used unit threshold	12	1	20%
Unit Bonus threshold	20	4	0

Date	Customer Name	Stock Number	Make	Model	New/Used	Gross	Pack	Gross (after pack)	Calculated Comm	Override	Final Comm
			Make A		New			0.00	0.00		0.00
			Make A		Used			0.00	0.00		0.00
			Make A		New			0.00	0.00		0.00
			Make B		New			0.00	0.00		0.00
								0.00	0.00		0.00
								0.00	0.00		0.00
								0.00	0.00		0.00
								0.00	0.00		0.00
								0.00	0.00		0.00
								0.00	0.00		0.00
								0.00	0.00		0.00
								0.00	0.00		0.00
								0.00	0.00		0.00
								0.00	0.00		0.00
								0.00	0.00		0.00
								0.00	0.00		0.00
								0.00	0.00		0.00
								0.00	0.00		0.00
								0.00	0.00		0.00
								0.00	0.00		0.00
								0.00	0.00		0.00
								0.00	0.00		0.00
								0.00	0.00		0.00
								0.00	0.00		0.00
								0.00	0.00		0.00
								0.00	0.00		0.00
								0.00	0.00		0.00
								0.00	0.00		0.00
								0.00	0.00		0.00
								0.00	0.00		0.00
										Unit Bonus	0.00
										Grand Total	0.00

This has been dressed up a little bit, partly for looks and partly for functionality. First of all, the gridlines were turned off by choosing Tools, Options, then on the View tab unchecking the Gridlines box.

The Salesperson, Test Table, and Detail areas were then added, along with borders and colors. The turquoise cells are user-entered, and the blue cells are calculations. (Note: this can be further enhanced by turning on protection in the workbook. To do that, you would select all the turquoise cells, then right-click, choose Format Cells, and on the Protection tab uncheck the Locked option. Once all the turquoise cells are formatted this way, you can click the Review tab, then

Protect Sheet (and either enter a password or not). You would then be able to access only the turquoise cells, leaving everything else protected from changes.)

You could build this page from scratch, but it's easier to study the sample workbook to see how this page is constructed. Here are some of the highlights:

In the Test Table area, the Threshold numbers were entered by selecting a cell (e.g. C7 for the Minimum commission amount), pressing the "=" key, then clicking on the Master page, moving your cursor to the Minimum commission amount (125), and pressing the Enter key. After you do that, the formula bar will display =Minimum_commission, and will always refer to the minimum commission amount on the Master page.

The Actual column counts the cars in the Detail area by using the COUNTIFS formula. Here's a sample line:

```
=COUNTIFS($E$14:$E$43,"Make A",$G$14:$G$43,"New")
```

Back in the olden days of Excel, the only way to create a formula like this was by means of what's called an array, and it could get really complicated. It's much easier now to create and understand. The formula simply counts how many vehicles there are if both "Make A" is in column E and "New" is in column G.

The next column in the Test Table is the percentage column. This represents the current percentage to use as the basis for calculation on any given record in the Detail area. These formulas make use of the range names we created from the Master sheet. For example:

```
=IF(D8<=Make_A_unit_threshold,Make_A_comm_up_to_threshold,Make_A_comm_above_threshold)
```

Here we're checking for the count of new Make A units sold, as reflected in cell D8. As new Make A records are added to the Detail area, the count in D8 will continue to increase. As long as the count stays less than or equal to 10, the formula in the percentage column will use the percentage in the range name
"Make_A_comm_up_to_threshold", which is 15%. As soon as the count hits 11 cars or more, the formula will switch to the value in range name
"Make_A_comm_above_threshold", which is 20%. All Make A cars in the Detail area will then recalculate at the higher percentage. The same logic holds true for Make B, used, and the unit threshold.

Now for our Detail area. As we pointed out, the turquoise area is for user input, the blue areas are our calculations. The Gross (after pack) column is a simple calculation subtracting the pack amount from the gross. Likewise, the Final Comm amount simply checks to see if the Override cell next to it is blank. If it's not (meaning we've had to enter one of those famous "Oh, I promised the salesperson x instead of y on that deal" numbers, then Excel will use that instead of the

Calculated Comm number as the final commission amount for that deal.

The Calculated Comm column is a bit more complicated in its formula. Here's an example (with line wrapped due to length):

```
=IF(OR(ISBLANK(E14),ISBLANK(G14),(ISBLANK(H14))),0,IF(G14="Used",IF(J14*$E$10<$
C$7,$C$7,J14*$E$10),IF(AND(E14="Make
A",G14="New"),IF(J14*$E$8<$C$7,$C$7,J14*$E$8),IF(AND(E14="Make
B",G14="New"),IF(J14*$E$9<$C$7,$C$7,J14*$E$9),0))))
```

Okay, I'll grant you, this is a bit frightening at first. But after we break it down into manageable chunks, you'll see its bark is bigger than its bite. Here's a more simplified way of looking at this formula:

If the Make OR Model OR Gross amount cell are blank, return a zero

BUT…

If all 3 are NOT blank (meaning we've made valid entries in all 3 cells), THEN…If the New/Used cell says "Used", THEN…if the gross amount times the percentage for used cars in the Test Table is less than our minimum commission amount, then give us our minimum commission amount. Otherwise, give us the calculated commission.

BUT…

If instead our Make cell says "Make A" and our New/Used cell says "New", THEN if our calculated gross is less than the minimum, give us the minimum, otherwise give us the calculated commission.

BUT...

If instead our Make cell says "Make B" and our New/Used cell says "New", THEN if our calculated gross is less than the minimum, give us the minimum, otherwise give us the calculated commission.

OTHERWISE...

Leave it at zero.

Written in more computer-language-program-eze, this is how the formula would look:

```
If Make = "" OR New/Used = "" OR GrossAmt = ""Then
    Answer = 0
ElseIfNewUsed = "Used" Then
    If CalculatedCommission<MinimumCommission Then
       Answer = MinimumCommission
    Else
       Answer = CalculatedCommission
    End If
Elself Make = "Make A" And NewUsed = "New" Then

    If CalculatedCommission<MinimumCommission Then
        Answer = MinimumCommission
    Else
        Answer = CalculatedCommission
    End If
Elself Make = "Make B" And NewUsed = "New" Then
```

```
If CalculatedCommission<MinimumCommission Then
   Answer = MinimumCommission
Else
   Answer = CalculatedCommission
End If
Else
   Answer = 0
End If
```

As you can see, Excel can pack a lot of processing into a relatively compact formula. This is the workhorse formula for the worksheet. It checks for all the conditions possible in order to arrive at the correct calculated commission amount. And as the car sale records increase in the Detail area, the formula will always return the correct result as it constantly checks the percentages in the Test Table.

Finally, at the bottom of the Detail area is our unit bonus cell, which simply reflects whatever shows up in the Test Table (0 or 500, depending on the total number of cars sold). Below that is our grand total, which adds up everything in the Final Comm column.

In order to use this workbook, you simply need to create a copy of the Template page for each salesperson. You can do that by pressing the Control key, then clicking the Template tab. When you see an image of a piece of paper with a plus sign, drag it next to the Template page. A new copy will be created, at which point you can double-click the tab name and rename it from Template(2) to the salesperson's name.

When you name the tab, even though Excel allows you to do this, I always recommend not using spaces in the tab name. For example, if the salesperson's name is John Smith, name the tab JohnSmith, or John_Smith (with an underscore instead of a space), or Smith_John, etc. While this isn't strictly necessary, you'll notice that tab names without spaces are a lot easier to deal with in macros than tab names that include spaces.

As you create each new tab and name it, enter the salesperson's name at the top of the sheet. You can use whatever format you want for the name here, since it's for reference purposes only.

If the terms of the commission pay plan change, such as the percentages or threshold quantity on any of the cars, you need only change it on the Master page. Because the Template (and thus the salesperson) page refers to the Master page for its information, all the changes will automatically flow to the supporting sheets.

In making use of the workbook on a monthly basis, you can first add your salespeople tabs and save the workbook as a template workbook, calling it something like commission.xlsx. Then you can open it for the new month, complete the workbook and save it with a unique file name, such as commission_202406.xlsx. Then for the next month simply open the template workbook and begin again.

Of course, the pay plan presented in this workbook is only a sample, and it's unlikely that it would be anything like the plan in your dealership. This is provided as a starting point for ideas on how you can build a workbook that reflects your dealership's plan, while keeping in mind the idea of flexibility and foundation.

Bonus Workbook - Excel to PDF

"Efficiency is doing better what is already being done."
- Peter F. Drucker

In our previous case study we built a commission workbook that runs on sheer calculation. Everything in it is self-contained, in that it consists of data entry regions and calculation regions. Range names, reference areas, array formulas and multiple-criteria IF statements combine to do everything necessary to make it a working spreadsheet. Because our key information is contained in a Master sheet and simply referenced in the salesperson tabs, we've created a spreadsheet that's easier to maintain. Any changes need only be made in one place instead of many.

This workbook could be the end result for us if that's all we want. But we could go further with it. We could incorporate it into a process that would save the office some time and get the information to the salespeople much more quickly.

This is where our bonus workbook comes into play. This workbooks is based on our previous commission.xlsx file, and it includes a code module that exports each salesperson worksheet as a PDF file into a selected folder on your computer. After all the worksheets have been exported, the PDF files can be printed and distributed or emailed to each salesperson.

Because some of the coding is a bit more advanced that what we've done up to this point, we won't be building the macro interactively. Instead, the code will be briefly explained below, and you can study it to see how you could apply this to other workbooks that you might want to use for exporting worksheets.

First off, here's the code module procedure:

```
Sub Export_Commission_Sheets()
    Dim SheetName As String
    Dim CurrentWorkbook As String
    Dim i As Integer
    Dim FilePath As String
    Dim CountFiles As Integer
    Dim fs
    Dim objFiles

    Set fs = CreateObject("Scripting.FileSystemObject")

FilePath = Range("ExportPath")
CurrentWorkbook = ActiveWorkbook.Name

    Set objFiles = fs.GetFolder(FilePath).Files
CountFiles = objFiles.Count

  If CountFiles> 0 Then
    If MsgBox(CountFiles& " files are already in the 'data' folder." & _
          "Click Yes to automatically delete them or No to stop this program", _
vbYesNo, "Automatically delete files") = vbNo Then
      Exit Sub
    Else
      On Error Resume Next
      Kill FilePath& "*.*"
      On Error GoTo 0
    End If
  End If
```

```
    For i = 1 To Sheets.Count
        If Sheets(i).Name <> "Master" And _
           Sheets(i).Name <> "Template" Then

SheetName = Sheets(i).Name

        Sheets(i).ExportAsFixedFormat Type:=xlTypePDF, Filename:= _
FilePath&SheetName& ".pdf", Quality:=xlQualityStandard, IncludeDocProperties _
        :=True, IgnorePrintAreas:=False, OpenAfterPublish:=False

    End If
  Next i

MsgBox ("All commission sheets exported")

End Sub
```

Some of the coding you will recognize from our earlier exercises, but some of it will be quite foreign to you unless you've programmed in VBA before.

The variable declarations at the top are easy to understand, with the exception of "fs" and "objFiles". These two variables will hold what's called the FileSystemObject. This is a programming object that allows us to manage files and folders more easily. If you want to learn more about the FileSystemObject, there are plenty of sources in the Microsoft support pages and even YouTube tutorial videos.

Once the FileSystemObject variables are loaded, they check for the existence of a data folder and whether there are files present in it. If so, they will delete any files prior to running the code.

After the housekeeping is done, the main portion of the macro counts the number of sheets in the workbook, and then runs through a loop (See the line: For I = 1 to Sheets.Count).

For every sheet in the workbook that is NOT named "Master" or "Template", (i.e., theoretically, it's a salesperson sheet), it saves the sheet as a PDF file in the chosen folder with the salesperson's name for the file. After looping through all the sheets, whether there's 1 or 100 salespeople, the macro finishes and displays a message. After that, you can close the workbook and distribute the PDF files either directly or by emailing them.

The only thing you'll need to do is make sure the Export File Path is entered on the Master worksheet and that's it's a valid path (Make sure to include the final backslash character in the file path.) Otherwise, you'll get an error when the macro tries to export the files.

Final Thoughts

I've lost track of how many custom Excel workbooks and VBA applications I've created over the years. As you can see from just the few examples above, Excel and VBA can be used to create powerful and flexible solutions to many problems in dealerships.

Frankly, VBA has gotten some bad rap almost from the start as a "toy" programming language. I couldn't disagree more with this. While VBA has its roots in the Basic programming language, it has developed over the years into a capable (and even formidable) language. When it comes to being able to do what you need it to in Excel in order to enhance Excel's capabilities, it's unlikely you'd run into its limits.

As for Excel itself, I'll wager that most people who use it have no idea how powerful it really is. If you really want to invest in the time to learn more about it and how you can use it in the dealership, there are almost endless resources, from books to teaching sites like Udemy to entire courses on YouTube.

One thing I will tell you though if you embark on becoming more proficient in Excel and even learning how to program it in VBA: Don't wait until some magical moment. It's human nature to start learning something more complex like this and think, "Okay, I'll read through this entire book, or I'll watch this entire video series, or I'll attend these seminars, and THEN I'll know enough to start building great spreadsheets." The problem is that time never comes. Trust me.Been there, done that.

I finally decided to just start building a simple program in VBA after I had spent way too much time trying to get book-smart about it, and it opened my eyes. Yes, it was gawd-awful ugly, and I'd be embarrassed to produce something like that now. But it was the start. It did what it needed to do. Once I realized I had actually built something useful, it become easier to keep going. My skills improved, my knowledge improved, and my spreadsheets became better over time. You have to take that first step to realize that you can become proficient in building Excel workbooks. And by the way, that applies to just about everything in life.

So, I encourage you to learn more about Excel and how it can help you in your business. It's one of the best investments you can make in your business and in yourself.

About the Author

Jack Ross worked in the dealership world from 1985 until his retirement in 2021. Starting out in payables and receivables, he went on to learn data entry on an IBM S/36. From there he learned computer programming on the IBM, then on personal computers with Lotus 1-2-3, relational database, and Excel and Reflection programming. He learned how to get under the hood, extracting data from the DMS in order to create customized reports for auditors and managers, and automation routines for departments to make their procedures faster and more efficient.

Jack served as chairman of the ADP (CDK) User Group #1 for Northeast Ohio/ Western Pennsylvania for several years and held seminars for Advanced ADP (CDK) Reflection. He also published articles on the Alpha Four relational database program in the semi-technical newsletter *Alpha Forum*

Jack now works as a freelance consultant at his own company, Grayfox Software, that has helped dealerships and 3rd party vendors with scripting and spreadsheet programming.

More information can be found at grayfoxsoftware.com.

9 7 9 8 8 7 1 2 4 0 5 2 6